The Mighty Few

The Mighty Few

Two First Hand Accounts by Confederate
Soldiers During the American Civil War

Reminiscences of a Private
of the First South Carolina Volunteer Infantry
Frank M. Mixson

and

Reminiscence of Four Years as a
Private Soldier of the Maryland Infantry
& Cavalry
John Gill

LEONAUR

The Mighty Few
Two First Hand Accounts by Confederate Soldiers During the American Civil War
Reminiscences of a Private of the First South Carolina Volunteer Infantry
by Frank M. Mixson
and
Private Soldier of the Maryland Infantry & Cavalry
by John Gill

First published under the titles
Reminiscences of a Private
and
Reminiscence of Four Years as a Private Soldier

Leonaur is an imprint
of Oakpast Ltd

ISBN: 978-1-78282-112-0 (hardcover)
ISBN: 978-1-78282-113-7 (softcover)

http://www.leonaur.com

Contents

Reminiscences of a Private

PRIVATE F. M. MIXSON,
Forty-five years after the war.

Contents

Dedication

Dedicated to the Sons and Daughters of "the Lost Cause," who should know of the valour, trials, suffering and privations of the noblest people and the grandest army that God ever put on this earth, so that *they too* can pass down to their children and their children's children a true history of the great deeds of this glorious Southland, for the cause and principles they loved so well and for which they suffered, bled and died.

The author.

Preface

In the summer of 1865 I first met Frank M. Mixson, the writer of these reminiscences. He was then a boy of eighteen summers, with four years of continuous service in the army of the Confederate States to his credit.

In that depressing time, when the old civilization of the South had been prostrated by the cyclone of war, when every hope seemed forever gone from the sky of the darkened future, he was full of the steady, unflinching courage of the Confederate Veteran, looking with unwavering faith to the resurrection that loyalty to principle, trust in the right and confidence in the destiny of the Anglo-Saxon would assure in the peace of the patient coming years.

Heroes of the Lost Cause were not then so scarce as now, and from time to time many of the older comrades of the boy soldier told me of his deeds of cool daring on the battle line, of mischievous life in the winter bound camps or on the weary march.

And so the years passed, but they did not dim the memories of those who had touched elbows with him from Charleston to Appomattox.

At my insistent request, he, now graying with years, wrote for publication in my paper these reminiscences, as told by the winter fireside to the grandchildren gathered under his roof tree in the holiday time. As I read them, feeling their pathos, realizing their value as giving pictures of the great conflict that no other actor in that red drama had penned or voiced, the thought mastered me that these memories were worthy of a larger audience than I could reach and that from the Lakes to the Gulf, from the Atlantic to the Pacific, they should find as equal welcome, rouse as equal interest in homes of the victors by the stars and stripes as among the conquered ones whose flag had been forever furled. So these reminiscences are given to the broader world just as he wrote them with the hand that knew better the handling of the musket than the holding of the pen.

Not a word or a syllable have I changed, not a thought have I suggested.

To those who read his plain, unvarnished story there will come a fuller understanding of the spirit of the old South than the cultured historians have written. The heart and hope of Dixie are laid bare to sight and feeling, the courage and endurance of the legions of Lee and Jackson, the patient, uncomplaining consecration of the women who kept the homes and fed and clothed the thin lines that so long held back such invincible odds. All in all, it is the best book of the many that I have read touching the war between the States. It gives an insight into the life and character of the Southern soldier that must appeal to every human heart not dead to chivalry and must win from those who were the bitterest foes of the South and its peculiar institutions a higher respect for and admiration of those once their enemies, but who have cast all hate from their hearts. It is a true history. I have verified by the testimony of as good men as breathe the air of South Carolina the truth and accuracy of the events described.

Faithful as a soldier in the brave young morning of his life, Private Mixson has in the afternoon of his years rendered a noble service to the South he loved so well and the cause he served as becomes a modern knight.

John W. Holmes,
Editor of *The People*.

Barnwell, S. C., March 5, 1910.

CHAPTER 1

I Join the First South Carolina Volunteers

The author of these reminiscences (F. M. Mixson) was born at Barnwell Court House, South Carolina, on the 5th day of December, 1846. I was the nineteenth and youngest child of Wm. J. and Sarah Ann Mixson. My father died when I was about six years old, leaving my mother a large family to see after. My father, Wm. J. Mixson, was recognized as one of the best men of Barnwell District and had the reputation of being one of the most truthful and honest and best men of the State. He was familiarly known in the District as "Uncle Billy," and his word was always taken without dispute. My mother, before her marriage, was Sarah Ann Johnston, from the lower part of Barnwell District, now Hampton County. She was highly connected with the best people of the lower section of the State. She was a woman of great business capacity, being very energetic, fine business ability and quite industrious. They married quite young and raised a large family.

Of my parents' families I know very little. My father had four brothers—Joyce, Charles, Archie and Miles—all of whom lived in the lower part of Barnwell District, between Johnston's Landing and Matthews' Bluff, on the Savannah River. They all had good sized families. Early in the 1850's they all moved to Florida with their families and that State is now thickly populated with Mixsons and Mixson descendants. Father also had four sisters. Aunt Experience married Ben Brown and afterwards Fogler. Aunt Susan also married a Brown (Josiah). Aunt Levisy married Robert Kirkland, of Buford's Bridge, and Aunt Hanson married James Darlington, of the Cypress Chapel section. All of these had families and were well to do in this world's goods.

My mother had, so far as I am informed, two brothers—Uncle Joe Johnston being the eldest. He remained in the State, his home being in the upper part of Beaufort District, now Hampton County. He, too, was well off in this world's goods. He at one time represented his District in the Legislature. In those times travel was not like now. When Uncle Joe would leave home for Columbia, the capital, he would mount one horse, his negro boy another with the hand-bag of wearing apparel. It would take them some three days to make the trip. Then was the time when the State House was a small wooden building situated on the same grounds as now.

The only place the members and public had to stop and put up was at Granby's—a high bluff on the Congaree River, about two and a half miles from the present State House, where there was a boarding house. Uncle Ben Johnston moved to Shreveport, La., before the war and amassed quite a fortune. Mother had three sisters—Aunt Charlotte married Amos Smart, Aunt Jerusha married Henry Best—both of the Allendale section—and Aunt Elizabeth married —— Worton, of Bainbridge, Ga. At the death of my father, mother immediately administered on the estate and she decided it best to take her share and have the children's portion put in the hands of guardians; consequently, she had everything sold, including about sixty-five negroes. This being converted into money, the guardians of those under age were placed in charge of it for their respective charges.

It happened to my fortunate lot to have as my guardian the Hon. James J. Wilson, then State Senator, and at that time a practicing attorney at the Barnwell Bar. He, however, did not remain long in Barnwell after taking me in charge, but returned to his plantation on the Four Mile section of Barnwell District, near the Savannah River, which is now the Ellenton section. I went with him and regarded that my home and was treated as a child by both Mr. and Mrs. Wilson, they having no children of their own except a grown son of Mr. Wilson's by a former marriage. I would occasionally go down to Barnwell to visit my mother and family, sometimes remaining for several weeks. I was truly fortunate in falling into the hands of these good people. Mr. Wilson was one of the best Christian gentlemen I have ever known, and during the many years I remained with him I never saw nor heard any word or act but that bespoke the true Christian, honest and lovable man; and Mrs. Wilson, too, was as kind as a mother to me, a good woman in every sense, but who spoiled me with kindness.

I cannot, even now at sixty-four years of age, forget their parental care and kindness to me. They have long ago gone to their reward, a place of peace and rest prepared for such as they were and so richly deserved by them.

The first year of Mr. Wilson's guardianship of me we spent in Barnwell. I was then quite young, but to keep me out of mischief, I suppose, I was sent to school in the village. This school was presided over by a Mr. H. Melville Myers, who taught in Barnwell for many years and died there at an advanced age.

On going up to the plantation on the Four Mile I did nothing for some time, but finally a new school house was built by the neighbourhood—the Bushes, Dunbars, Williams, Newmans, Wilsons, and perhaps one or two others, and a Mr. R. H. Alfred, a Campbellite preacher, was engaged to take us in charge. Mr. Alfred was a fine scholar and teacher, and a perfect gentleman. This school house was built about four miles from my home and I had to walk alone. This would seem hard these times, but then it was not so much. This school ran for more than a year, when, for some cause, it closed. In the meantime, my mother had sold out her belongings in Barnwell and purchased a plantation ten miles above Barnwell, on the Hamburg Road, and known then and now as Joyce's Branch.

In the summer of 1860, there being no school on the Four Mile, and my sister Sarah, now Mrs. Richmond, of Atlanta, having a school at Joyce's Branch Church, I went down home and went to school to her; but she gave up the school in the fall and was succeeded by Mr. McBride, an old teacher of much note, who had taught so long that he knew every sum in the arithmetic by heart. At this time came the excitement of secession, minute men, war *and the big comet*—all on us at one time. I had no time for anything else, and attended every meeting of every kind. A company of minute men was organized with Dr. Frederick as commander.

This I joined, though not yet fourteen years old. We had our meetings every Saturday at Fred Killingsworth's, near Cypress Chapel Church, for the purpose of drill and to talk over the events that were happening and things *we knew would* happen in the very near future. I tell you, I was proud of my cockade and wore it on every occasion. This company was not formed with the idea of going into service as a company, but for the purpose of meeting together, talk over matters and keep enthused. I am proud to say, however, that when the call was made to enlist in companies that every member of our Minute Men responded like patriots and joined some command. I had then reached about fourteen years, and, while I had been admitted a member of the Minute Men, there was no company that was being organized that would consent to take me in, especially as I could not get the consent of my mother and Mr. Wilson. This, however, did not dampen my enthusiasm, for I just knew if I did not get there on time the Yankees would "*lick*"*us in short order,* hence, I determined to go whenever the troops were ordered out, consent or no consent.

About the first of the year 1860 I returned to the Four Mile. I found that during my absence at my mother's a young physician—Dr. Martin Bellinger—had located in that section and had taken board at our house; and also a nephew of Mrs. Wilson's had lately come to study law under Mr. Wilson. I made fast friends with both these gentlemen, especially Dr. Bellinger. Mr. Steve Laffitte was the name of the law student. He not having much to do, and I nothing, he took me in charge for instruction, but neither of us did much. There was also staying at our house a great big Irishman, by name John Nicholson, a true son of Erin. It goes without saying that Nicholson and I were the very best of friends.

The war talk continued and companies were being raised. Nicholson volunteered in a company being raised by Capt. Wm. J. Crawley. This company was assigned to Holcombe Legion when ordered out. I do not remember the date, but the company was ordered to report and get together at Williston, S. C., at a certain time. I slept with Nicholson his last night home, and next morning I arose before daylight, without breakfast or anything to eat, with no clothing—with nothing but enthusiasm. I headed off for Williston, a distance of twenty-seven miles, *a-foot.* I expected, however, that the wagons containing the men would overtake me during the morning. I had gotten perhaps as far as three miles on my way, walking leisurely along, meditating on the life of a soldier, the many battles I would be in, the gallant deeds I would do, and, above all, the host of Yankees I would kill and put to flight, when I heard the tramp of a horse's feet coming up from the rear.

I intuitively knew what it was, but, deigning to look back, I continued my onward course. The horseman soon overtook me, and, riding by me until he got to a pine stump on the side of the road, he rode up to it and waited for me, and on my approach, he (Mr. Wilson) said, "Get up," which I did, and we retraced our way for home. Not another word but "get up" was said during the whole time. I felt that I was being badly treated, and I had the sulks, and Mr. Wilson, in the goodness of his heart, spared me the humility of a lecture.

There were other companies being formed which were to form Hagood's First South Carolina, and it was not many days before they, too, were ordered to rendezvous at Orangeburg, S. C. I had in the meantime gone down to my mother's; she thought the best thing for me was to be put to the plough. This she did. I had been ploughing only a few days—perhaps only two days—when in the morning a wagon came along loaded with men on their way to Barnwell to join Hagood there and go from there to Orangeburg, where the famous Hagood's First South Carolina Volunteers were organized. I did nothing less than drive my horse in a fence, jam and load myself on that wagon.

Arriving at Barnwell, Johnson Hagood met us, and, looking us over, he spied me and said, "Frank, go back home. Too small now; you will do later." There was nothing else for me to do but get back again. This was some time about the first of April, 1861. About two months after this, I could just stand it no longer, and off I go again without saying a word to anyone. I went to Charleston and over to the Regiment and joined Company I, commanded by Capt. J. J. Brabham, in which my brother, J. S. Mixson, was first lieutenant. When Hagood saw me down there he again ordered me home, and I told him I had already joined. Besides, if he drove me away I would go somewhere else and join. He let up, and I was happy beyond measure. The regiment at that time was only twelve months' troops, and during the fall and winter the reorganization for the war commenced.

In the reorganisation Company I became Company C, with B. B. Kirkland as Captain. My brother, J. S., did not re-enlist, but went to a cavalry company serving on the coast and became quartermaster sergeant of the regiment. I remained with Company C for over a year, when Ely Myrick, of Company E, and I exchanged, he going to Company C, Capt. Kirkland, and I to Company E, Capt. Wood. There was in Company E my eldest brother, Joyce, between whom and myself there were seventeen children—his son, G. D. Mixson, and two Nelson boys, who were my nephews, all of whom were several years older than I. We were stationed on Coles Island during the winter of 1861, but after the reorganisation we were moved to James Island and remained there till we were ordered to Virginia.

Brother John and his two sons, Elliott and Adrian, re-enlisted in Hunter's Company, Lamar's Second Artillery, and remained in South Carolina and saw hard service on James Island. While on James Island I would get a pass to Charleston whenever I could and spend the day with my sister Susan, who was Sister Mary Magdeline, in the Sisters of Mercy, and on every visit I was treated right royally by them. I remember that before leaving for Virginia my sister placed something around my neck, and until the string wore out and I lost it I was never hurt, but the first fight I went into after losing this I was wounded.

CHAPTER 2

Manassas

I failed to mention that before the reorganisation of the regiment for the war Johnson Hagood had been promoted to Brigadier General and was in command on James Island; and I also failed to say that James Hagood, a Citadel boy of about 17½ years, and a brother of the General, had come over to James Island and joined Company C, Capt. B. B. Kirkland, as a private. We were taken over to Charleston and encamped on the Citadel Green, preparatory to leaving for Virginia. Just after getting over to Charleston I was taken with "low country fever," and was sent up to the hospital in Augusta, Ga. Old Dr. Ford was in charge of the hospital, which was the old Eagle and Phoenix Hotel. I was up there about three weeks when I heard that the regiment had left Charleston for Virginia. I immediately went to Dr. Ford and asked for a discharge from the hospital and transportation to Richmond, where I hoped to overtake them.

He tried to dissuade me from leaving, and offered me a permanent place under him, but I did not go into service to hang up in hospitals, consequently, I declined and got my discharge and transportation and took the first train going North. I was alone—had never been out of the State, except to Augusta—a mere kid of a boy. I can tell you, I felt mighty lonesome. Besides, I was afraid that the regiment would get so far ahead of me that I would not overtake them before they got to the fighting ground. I felt that if the regiment did get in a fight without me I would forever be disgraced, no matter the reason. Fortunately, just before reaching Richmond I ran up on Dr. Martin Bellinger, our surgeon, who had been looking after some sick before leaving Charleston, and who, too, had got behind.

We got to Richmond about four days after the regiment had left for Manassas. Dr. Bellinger's horse was there, but I had to take it a-foot and alone, except some stragglers, like myself, none of whom, however, did I know, as they were not from our regiment. Dr. Bellinger, in Richmond, took me to the Spotswood Hotel and gave me dinner, after which we both left to overtake our men. It was just outside the city when the doctor rode away from me. I felt that I was deserted by everybody and disgraced if I let the regiment get into a fight before I reached them. I travelled that night until about midnight, when I lay down by the roadside and slept till sunrise. I again pulled out and kept on the go.

By this time the rations that I had slipped into my haversack at the Spotswood were gone. I did not know how I would get something to eat from then on. In passing by a pasture I saw four or five sheep. I loaded my musket, took deliberate aim at one not more than twenty steps off, fired and *missed*. I shot at this old fellow not less than five times and gave it up in disgust. That evening, just before sundown, I ran across a large, fat hog. I know it could not have weighed less than three hundred pounds. I was hungry good by this time, and I was determined to have meat. I loaded up and first fire *brought her down*. I then skinned and cut off a ham, and going perhaps a mile further, I stopped for the night at a spring by the roadside. The balance of the hog I left where she fell; but as I had passed so many stragglers I know she did not spoil, for they, like myself, were hungry.

I feasted that night on broiled ham—no salt, no bread, *but it was good*. This ham lasted me until I overtook the wagon train, which was about six miles in rear of the regiment, or, I may say now, the army. I overtook these wagons in camp about twelve o'clock at night and I stopped to camp. I was very much surprised to be awakened perhaps an hour before day by the firing of cannon and small arms ahead. I could not remain longer. I got up and headed for the front. Not being experienced in warfare at that time, I had no idea that the firing on the front was exceeding three miles at most, but when I came to travel it I found that after I had gone at least six miles I had only reached the location of the field hospital. Here again I ran upon Dr. Bellinger, he having very little help, and with a desire to care for me, as he saw that I was about broken down, he ordered me to remain to assist with the wounded, who had begun to come in. I protested, but he held firm and I was soon at work.

The duty demanded of me by Dr. Bellinger was to assist in the examinations and amputations, and many a poor fellow did I hold while his leg or arm was taken off. I was shocked at the number of our regiment brought back killed and wounded. Men whom I had only a few weeks before left in Charleston in the best of health and spirits, some dead, others wounded. I could hardly realize such carnage. Over half of the regiment was killed and wounded. I remained with Dr. Bellinger until the wounded were all disposed of, when he let me go. I overtook the regiment just after they crossed the Potomac River into Maryland.

Our regiment left Charleston and went into the Manassas fight with Thos. J. Glover, of Orangeburg, Colonel; Wm. H. Duncan, of Barnwell, Lieutenant-Colonel; Daniel H. Livingston, of Orangeburg, Major; Wm. J. Wood, of Steel Creek, Adjutant; Mortimer Glover, of Orangeburg, Sergeant-Major; Captain Warren B. Flowers, of Baldoc, Quartermaster; (I cannot recollect now who was the commissary); Dr. Martin Bellinger, of Four Mile, Surgeon; Dr. Wm. S. Stoney, of Allendale, Assistant Surgeon. The Company Commanders were: Company A, Capt. Isaac Bamberg, Bamberg; Company B, Capt. —— Wannamaker, Orangeburg; Company C, Capt. B. B. Kirkland, Buford's Bridge; Company D, Capt. Robt. L. Crawford, Marion; Company E, Capt. Jno. H. Thompson, Upper Three Runs; Company F, Capt. T. D. Gwinn, Greenville; Company G, Capt. J. G. Grimes, Bamberg; Company H, Capt. John C. Winsmith, Spartanburg; Company I, Capt. Jas. H. Stafford, Marion; Company K, Capt. —— Knotts, Orangeburg.

The lieutenants of the companies I cannot recollect. Gus Hagood, of Barnwell, was colour bearer. This is about the manner our regiment was officered on reaching Lee's army, and was assigned to Hood's Texas Brigade. We went into the Second Manassas about fourteen hundred strong. It seemed to me that every minute there was some poor fellow brought back. Col. Glover was killed outright. Maj. Livingston wounded slightly; Adjutant Wood wounded; Capt. Bamberg, of Company A, wounded; Capt. Wannamaker, Company B, wounded; Capt. Kirkland, Company C, wounded; Capt. Crawford, Company D, wounded; Capt. Thompson, Company E, killed; Capt. Gwinn, Company F, wounded; Capt. Grimes, Company G, wounded; Capt. Winsmith, Company H, wounded; Capt. Stafford, Company I, wounded; Capt. Knotts, Company K, wounded.

Besides these nearly all the lieutenants were either killed or wounded and about one-half, at least, of the regiment. You will therefore see that our regiment suffered very heavily. Our colours, *they say*, went down seven times. First, Gus Hagood was shot through the body, and Dr. Bellinger passed a silk handkerchief entirely through his body, taking hold of each end and wiping out the blood. He got well, but was never fit for service again.

As Hagood fell with the colours, Gus Eaves, from Bamberg, one of the colour guards, rushed to them and raised them aloft. In a few minutes his right arm was torn to splinters. Immediately they were seized by another,and this was continued until the eighth man bore them through. The fight continued from early morning till night, when the army camped on the battlefield, ready to renew next morning; but next morning the enemy had disappeared. We had been driving them all day.

Our regiment made charge after charge, and at one time during the day in making a charge and in passing over some wounded Yankees, one inquired, "What regiment is that?" and on being told "the First S. C. V.," he said, "You all are the d——st fools I ever saw; you have been whipped all day."

Nothing being in our front next day to hinder us, we arranged—each company—for its senior officers to command, in a great many instances, non-commissioned officers taking command, and we went on a chase into Maryland. Lieut.-Col. Duncan assumed command of the regiment and Maj. Livingston, who was only slightly hurt, returned to us just as we crossed the Potomac River. The first place I recollect after getting into Maryland was Frederick City. As we passed through the town everybody was out to see us; streets crammed, doors and windows full; some cheering and waving Confederate flags; others jeering us and waving United States flags. We went through the town in a "hurrah" and let them know that we knew we had just given the Yankee army a good licking at Manassas and were ready for them again.

Just after crossing into Maryland Lieut.-Col. Duncan, who was commanding our regiment since the killing of Col. Glover at Manassas, was taken sick and went back into an ambulance, but did not leave us entirely until we again crossed the Potomac back into Virginia, when he got a sick furlough and went home to Barnwell. This left the command of the regiment to Maj. Livingston. I was then orderly for the colonel, which required me to be at regimental headquarters and around the regimental commander at all times and to extend his private orders and commands. In this position I was not required to carry a gun, and it was well for me that I was so exempted, for I could never have made the marching had I been loaded down.

Before crossing into Maryland the entire army were ordered to leave all their baggage, and on this trip we had nothing but a haver-sack, canteen and a blanket or oil cloth, besides the accoutrements—gun, cartridge box and scabbard. You will see from this that we were prepared for *quick marching*.

CHAPTER 3

Slaughter at Sharpsburg

We took the turnpike from Frederick City to Hagerstown, and along the route we passed many an orchard heavily laden with fine apples and many corn fields with luscious roasting ears; but we were not allowed to gather a thing and rations were short. But at every cross road we would find a lot of ladies with tables set with something to eat and coffee and buckets of water. It was impossible for them to feed us all, but what they did do helped out considerably and was highly appreciated. We passed through Hagerstown at midday and went into camp in an oak grove some two miles beyond the town. In passing through Hagerstown all the stores remained open and none of the citizens seemed to be in the least uneasy. As we were going down the street we saw a corner store with the sign "Hager's Store."

Standing in the doors of this store were a *lot* of women and some children. Among them was a young girl some sixteen years old, who was waving a United States flag and taunting us with "Why don't you fight under this flag?" Some fellow in ranks remarked, "Hagerstown, Hager's store, Hager's daughter—hurrah for Hager," and, as was the custom, we gave them the yell. We remained in this grove outside the town until the next day after midday, when the "long roll" called us to "fall in." We were again marched through the town, this time in a *double quick*, and took the turnpike for Boonesboro Gap, where we could hear heavy musketry and cannonading going on.

It was about sixteen miles from where we were camped to the gap, and as we were needed there badly we double quicked nearly the entire distance. Of course, we were stopped a few minutes at intervals to rest and catch our breath. It seems that this gap was the only way we had to get back into Virginia, and the Yankees were trying to hold this against us. Had they succeeded in doing this, Lee's army would

26

be trapped, but our troops held them at bay until Jenkins' Brigade got there about deep dusk. We found our troops hard pressed on the side of the mountains only a few hundred yards from the pass. We were immediately put into position and relieved those who had been fighting all day. Our orders were to hold our position or die.

After being in position here for some little time and holding the enemy back, an officer rode up to near where Maj. Livingston and I were and asked for the commanding officer. I hollered out, "Here he is." He told Maj. Livingston that the enemy were being reinforced and would charge us very shortly, and to save the pass long enough for our army to succeed in getting by, that we would *charge first*—that the orders to charge had been extended on our right and all movements would be taken up from the right. Maj. Livingston turned to me and said, "Frank, tell Company A to move as the regiment on its right moves, and come on down the line and tell each company commander to move as the right moves."

I had hardly got the orders extended before I heard the command, "Company A, forward," "Company B, forward." And on down the line. We were in for it sure, and away we went—into a blaze of musketry which lighted us on our way. We drove them back some little distance and held our gain long enough for the rear of our army to pass through, when we again heard the right extending orders. This time I heard, "Company A in retreat," "Company B in retreat," and it was not long before we were going through the gap—*the last of the army to pass through*. We found a relief for us when we got through, which held them back till we were safe on our road to Sharpsburg, which we reached sometime late in the afternoon, after having been fighting nearly all night and marching since noon the day before.

On reaching Sharpsburg we were stopped in an apple orchard (our regiment) and we fared well. We remained in this orchard that night, all next day and night. The second morning about sunrise the Yankees opened their artillery from the heights on us, and it seemed as if they had placed all the cannon *in the world* up there; it was certainly the heaviest and most terrific artillery firing during the entire war, and has gone down in history as such. Fortunately for us we were in a bottom and the worst of the shells went over us, but not all. We had a good many hurt while in this position. Our batteries were on the hill above us and were responding all they could.

About 8 o'clock we were ordered up the hill to protect our batteries; the enemy were charging them. We went up the hill at a double quick. Our regiment was on the left of the brigade and we were going left in front, which put us to the front. I was trotting by the side of Maj. Livingston amid a furore of bursting shells. About half way up the hill Maj. Livingston called to me, saying, "Lead on, Frank, I am wounded." I called to Capt. Knotts, who was the senior captain present, and told him to take command of the regiment. We got in position on the hill in rear of a plank fence and were told not to fire a shot till ordered to do so.

While lying behind the fence the Yankees were making their charge and coming down the opposite hill in as pretty a line as on dress parade. In front of us, and about midway, there was a stone fence in another apple orchard. The Yankees were making for this fence, and, as I said before, were moving on it at a double quick and a regular dress parade line. The old captain commanding our batteries had shot himself out of balls, and, all his horses being killed, he ordered his men to cut off the trace chains. With these he loaded his pieces and fired. It seemed that as the chains reached the ranks they spread themselves out full length and cut their way broadside through. The old captain jumped up, yelled, and ordered another load, with about the same result. This was done several times, and finally the column began to waver and weaken.

At this point a Yankee colonel rode to the front with drawn sword and rallied his men, who were about to give way. Just then I said to Kite Folk, from Bamberg, a boy like myself, but a year or two older, "Let us shoot him." I picked up a gun lying near me and Kite and I put our guns through the fence and fired together. The colonel fell and was carried from the field. The enemy fell back, but very soon came again.

Forty-two years after this occurrence I was running the Hotel Aiken. I was telling of this incident one evening when a guest of the house, who had registered as —— Johnson, said he knew the circumstance perfectly—that he was the major of that regiment and when the colonel was killed, as stated, he took command and received his promotion as lieutenant-colonel; that it was he who led them back in the second charge. When the enemy made this second charge we, too, made a charge, and the stone fence, spoken of before, being about equal distance from each of us, it was a race, who and who. We won the race, and when we fell in behind the fence the Yankees were not more than fifteen steps away; but it was not long before they had moved off, leaving a good crowd behind lying on the field. Could one have been so situated on one of these hills with nothing to do but witness the two forces making for that fence, the Yankees coming down the hill on their side, moving in line as if on drill, determination on their faces and a quick, steady step without a falter or a quaver—on the other hill a lot of dirty, hungry, footsore, naked and barefoot men lying behind that plank fence awaiting orders.

Soon the order came, and we were told to get to that stone fence. *No line for us.* Darling Patterson, of Barnwell, was our colour bearer, and he led off with our flag waving overhead. The men followed, each one doing all he could to get there first. We beat them to it, and when Patterson stuck his flag staff into the ground we had the fence, and too well did they know it. We tore loose into them, they not being more than fifteen steps distant. They could not stand it—they broke in confusion and retired in about the same order that we had advanced; but they were soon rallied and we had it hot for some time. The fence, however, was a great protection to us.

We were well protected by our stone fence in the apple orchard, but the enemy kept us pretty well engaged in our front, and we had no time to look around and see how other parts of our line were doing. We had been fighting behind this fence for perhaps two or three hours when I was surprised on looking around to see a long Georgia captain running from where we had come in the morning, and coming directly to me. I was then standing up under an apple tree eating an apple. On reaching me he said, "Where is your gun, and why are you not shooting?"

I replied, "I am the colonel's orderly." He then asked for the colonel. I told him that the regiment was right then without anyone to command it. He told me to get them back—the entire line had fallen back to our previous position—that we were the only ones so advanced, and to look to the right, coming from the direction of the barn, and I would see we were about already surrounded. I yelled out, "First South Carolina, retreat," and I led off.

The enemy were so close in our rear when we left the fence that we had to run *around* the *head of their column;* but every man succeeded in passing around them. But then we had a long, sloping hill to go up—nothing to break the view—an open field. Away we went, and while I was doing all I knew how in the way of running, and when I had about covered half the distance back, I ran up on Talt Best, from Allendale, lying flat on his back, shot through the thigh. He had lain there for several hours, being shot down when we advanced. Talt was holding out his arms and asked me piteously, "Frank, don't leave me here to die." It looked like death to me to stop, but I could not resist the appeal. I stooped down, raised him up. Just then Sid Key, from Joyce's Branch, ran up and I asked Sid to help me get Talt off. We got him back to our former line, where we turned him over to the litter bearers, and we got to our positions. We had not been there over five minutes when Sid Key was shot.

We received orders to prepare to advance, and I recollect Lieut. Jack Stansell, of Company E, waving his sword, cried out, "Forward, Company E." After repeating this several times and getting no response he discovered that he had but one man left in Company E, Arthur Thompson, of Elko. He then cried, "Forward, Thompson, go it, Thompson." Almost simultaneously a minnie ball passed through Thompson's body and a piece of shell hit Lieut. Stansell on the side of the knee. Both were carried off, and they were the last men of Company E.

After getting quieted down enough to look around I commenced to see who we could get to take command of the regiment. I have already told you that Capt. Knotts was placed in command when Maj. Livingston told me he was wounded. I could not find Capt. Knotts, nor had seen him the whole time of our advance while we were holding the stone fence. I think I may have failed to say heretofore that Jim Hagood had been appointed sergeant-major to fill the place of Mortimer Glover, of Orangeburg. In looking around for a regimental commander I discovered that there was only one commissioned officer left in the regiment. This officer was Lieut. Sweat, of Bamberg. I told him he would have to command the regiment, being the only officer. He refused to do so, and, after some thought, he told me to go to Sergt.-Major Jim Hagood and tell him to assume command. This I did, and Jim Hagood, a non-commissioned officer and an eighteen-year-old boy, took the command.

We held our ground the balance of the day and that night, and about daybreak next morning we passed through Sharpsburg and recrossed the Potomac into Virginia. While we were holding our ground on the battlefield about midnight the cooks came up with some cooked rations. Hagood sent me to ascertain how many men each company had left, so as to divide equally. I recollect Company E had *not one* and Company F only one. So, you see, we were right badly used up.

CHAPTER 4

Winter Quarters

After holding our ground and showing our enemy that we were not beaten at Sharpsburg, we left the battlefield in broad daylight and leisurely took our way to the Potomac and recrossed into Virginia. We stopped over at Martinsburg and then went on, and went into camp at the Big Spring, near Winchester, where we remained for three or four weeks. Here our baggage came to us and it was refreshing to get into clean clothes once more. While here a good many of our sick and slightly wounded returned to us, among whom was Maj. Livingston, who relieved Sergt.-Major Hagood in commanding the regiment. Nothing unusual occurred during our stay at the Big Spring, only that it was a good country to forage in and we usually had enough to eat and sometimes some apple jack to wash it down. After we had been at the Big Spring for several weeks, and the army had increased considerably, we were taken on a forced march and carried to Culpeper Court House. Here we remained for several weeks, again getting in more men who had recovered from wounds and sickness.

At this place Sergt.-Major Jas. Hagood was made adjutant. While remaining over here we had drills and dress parade every day and rested up pretty well. One day I got a pass to go over to Culpeper and took it up to brigade headquarters to have it countersigned. When Adjutant-General R. M. Simms saw my name he asked me if I knew Seth Mixson, of Barnwell, and when I said "He is my brother," Gen. Jenkins asked where he was. I told him on the coast. Gen. Jenkins then told me to write him. If he would accept he would have him appointed colonel of our regiment. You can imagine I was very much elated at this and wrote him immediately. In a short time I received a reply saying:

Tell Micah Jenkins I am quartermaster-sergeant of a cavalry regiment on the coast and would not give it for a major-general in Lee's army.

I was completely disgusted with the answer and never delivered it to Gen. Jenkins.

It was here that Col. Coward took command of the Fifth South Carolina. I recollect how game he looked. He had the regiment formed for dress parade. He was dressed in a brand new suit, polished high top boots, shining spurs and bright sword. He did not weigh over one hundred and twenty pounds, but he looked game. He had the orders read appointing him colonel, and then he told the men that he was now their colonel and would be respected as such; he would not tell them to go only as he led them. When he got through his talk the Fifth knew they had a colonel, and after-events proved it, for from then on the Fifth was one of the best regiments in our brigade. Before leaving here Lieut.-Col. Duncan was promoted to colonel and Maj. Livingston to lieutenant-colonel.

After some three weeks' stay here we were hurried over to Fredericksburg, reaching there in time to meet Hooker's advance. Upon reaching Fredericksburg our brigade was held in reserve for a time—in fact, for the entire day. About sundown we were moved up and relieved some troops that had been engaged, and we fought then nearly all night and the next day, until Hooker fell back across the river, leaving us in possession of the battlefield. After the enemy had recrossed the river we were taken to woods just off of the field, where we remained in position, ready for an attack at any moment, should they make an advance. We did not move back to these woods till about dark, consequently, during the afternoon we and the enemy were very near together, with the Rappahannock River only between us, but no fighting going on. Just before sundown the Yankee band came down to the river bank and commenced to play.

Very soon our bands were on the bank on our side. The Yankee band would play the popular airs of theirs amid much yelling and cheering; our bands would do the same with the same result. Towards the wind-up the Yankee band struck up "*Yankee Doodle.*" Cheers were immense. When they stopped our band struck up "*Dixie,*" and everything went wild. When they finished this, both bands, with one accord and simultaneously, struck up "*Home, Sweet Home.*" There was not a sound from anywhere until the tune was finished and it then seemed as if everybody had gone crazy. I never saw anything to compare with it. Both sides were cheering, jumping up and throwing up hats and doing everything which tended to show enthusiasm. This lasted for at least a half hour. I do believe that had we not had the river between us that the two armies would have gone together and settled the war right there and then.

I saw old weather-beaten men, naked, barefooted, hungry, dirty and worn out, with tears streaming down their cheeks; men who were not afraid to leave their homes, their wives, their families, their *all*; but men with hearts, who could not restrain the tears when it was so vividly brought to them. Their hearts were touched then, but they were yet men who were willing to do or die.

As before said, the army was taken back to the shelter of the woods, off the field of carnage, for the night. Company E of our regiment was left on the river bank to watch the movement of the enemy. I was left with them to carry any message to the colonel during the night, should the emergency arise. Some time, about two o'clock, there was considerable commotion in the camp of the enemy. Capt. Wood ordered me to report to the colonel that he thought they were preparing to make an advance. It was nearly a mile back to our line, raining and dark. I had to go across this battlefield alone, but there was no escape. I took a direct course. There was no woods on my way.

You nor no one can imagine how trying it was. One second I would stumble over a dead man or horse, next would step on some poor wounded fellow, who would either curse me or beg piteously for water or help; next run on a wounded horse and run the risk of being kicked to death. *It was fearful*; but after a time I reached the woods and delivered my message. The colonel instructed me to return and keep him informed. I told him, and begged him not to send me back before daylight—*I could not go*; it was *too much for me*. He took pity on me and allowed me to remain till daylight. I do believe that had he insisted on my returning that night that I would have died before making the trip.

There was no advance made by the enemy, but they moved off and went into winter quarters. This was the winter of 1862, and our first in Virginia; besides, it was a remarkably cold winter. They gave us little A tents, allowing six to a tent. We cut down trees and built up a pole house about three feet high, and pitched our tent on top of this, and when we had completed a chimney and had daubed the cracks with clay we had a very comfortable residence. Our great trouble was getting in wood; but we would take turn about to get in a day's supply. We fared very well, taking everything into consideration. There was a very heavy snow storm; snow fell about waist deep over the whole country.

One morning a few men commenced to snowball. These were added to until the whole army was engaged. Brigadier-generals took command of their brigades; colonels of their regiments; captains of their companies. It was a regular planned battle and was fought all day. Sometimes one would take the camp of another and plunder it of blankets, rations, cooking utensils and whatever else there was. It was the biggest snow ball fight on record. I did not engage in the fight, but took a hand in plundering a camp whenever we got into one. I had rations for several days after this affair—rations taken from the fellows' dinner out of their camps.

While here this winter we had a good many changes. Col. Duncan resigned and F. W. Kilpatrick, of Pendleton, was made colonel. Capt. Knotts, of Company K, resigned, and Jim Hagood was made captain of his company. S. B. Clowney, of Fairfield, was made adjutant. O. D. Wilson, of Allendale, was made sergeant-major, and other changes in company officers which I do not recall, except that P. H. Wood, of Steel Creek, was made captain of Company E. We remained in winter quarters until the severe winter was over, and when we had recruited so that our regiment and brigade had gotten to be quite respectable in size. When we broke winter quarters we were carried down on the Blackwater River, in the neighbourhood of Suffolk. I think Jenkins' Brigade was the only force carried down.

Our brigade was pretty badly scattered down here and had to cover a big space. The regiments were camped some four miles apart. After remaining here on the Blackwater for some little time the brigade was consolidated, and we were moved down to Suffolk. Here we were in daily communication with the enemy and our picket lines were only a short distance apart. While here we were one day asked for volunteers to go down and charge the gun boats. The volunteers were soon procured, but we wondered how infantry could charge gun boats. However, we went, and when we got in good range they opened on us with shells about the size of flour barrel heads. We did not make much out of charging gun boats.

We had several engagements with the enemy while in this section, holding back any advance they prepared to make and guarding Richmond from this direction. While here the Chancellorsville fight came off and it was here that we heard of the killing of Stonewall Jackson. The Chancellorsville fight was the only fight of any note that we had missed since we reached Virginia.

We remained down in this country until the spring had advanced and summer was about on us, when we were taken up to Petersburg and camped outside of the town and did police duty in the town. We were given new uniforms while here and fixed up in pretty good shape. Again we were fortunate, for while we were remaining here Lee made his advance into Pennsylvania and the great battle of Gettysburg was fought and we lost. Just after this battle when Lee saw Jenkins he said to him, "Jenkins, if I had had your brigade at Gettysburg I would have won."

This was high praise, but then we deserved it and it did not detract from any that were there. It was not long before we heard that Longstreet's corps was to go West and we got orders to pack up and move. We were loaded on freight trains in and on top of freight boxes at Petersburg, our brigade being the last of Longstreet's corps to leave.

CHAPTER 5

Chattanooga

Jenkins' brigade had been at Petersburg for some time after coming up from around Suffolk on the Blackwater and elsewhere down in that section, when we received orders to prepare to load and ship for the West with the balance of Longstreet's corps. Our brigade, however, was the last to be loaded and shipped, and we finally went to the depot and were loaded on freight boxes, inside and outside, the top being as much crowded as the inside. The trains those days did not make as good time as today, and, while I do not recollect how slowly we did run, I do recollect that when our regiment (the First South Carolina Volunteers) reached Bamberg and found the little town all lit up with bonfires and tables spread and the whole country—men, women and children—with baskets of cold chicken, rice pilau, biscuits, hams, boiled eggs, fried ham, salads and everything else that women can get up in a country of plenty, awaiting us and greeting us (the regiment) as if we were all their brothers; it made us feel good; and then Col. Kilpatrick, who was in charge of this train, held it for about an hour to give us time to do justice to what was tendered us.

Here it was that many an old fellow met his people for the first time since he had left them; even some here met their wives and children for the first time, and here I met one of my sisters who was visiting in the neighbourhood. I had not seen any of them since I first went. You may talk of courage and a sense of duty, but when a man pulls up at a station at 1 o'clock at night, finds there his wife and children whom he has not seen for two years, and after about one hour to see them, to be caressed by them, to be allowed to talk with them, then to be hauled off on a freight car—perhaps the only place for him on top—*that is manhood*. But this occurred in Bamberg, not in one case only, but in many—*they were men in those days*.

We passed through Denmark (then Graham's Turn Out), Lees, Blackville, Elko, Williston and White Pond. At each place some member of the regiment had loving friends and families, but no stop-over was allowed, and these old soldiers passed by their homes, outwardly showing cheerfulness, but one could discover their eyes were dim. We stopped over a couple of hours in Augusta, where we were transferred to the Georgia Road. We arrived in Atlanta early next morning and thence direct on to Chattanooga. It was right cold riding in and on top of freight boxes, so after leaving Atlanta we gathered some sand while the train was stopped and put it on the floor of the car, and on top, too, and that evening between sundown and dark we passed through Marietta with fires in and on top, cooking supper. We even spread down our beds on top of these trains and went regularly to bed.

We reached the nearest station to Chickamauga that was in our possession, and were immediately unloaded and ordered in a double quick for the battlefield. The fight had been going on since early the day before and Longstreet's corps had reached there to be in time, with the exception of our brigade. There was hard fighting at Chickamauga, and the battle was won when our brigade got in at a double quick. The enemy were already on the run, and we, being fresh, there was a regular stampede. Had Bragg let Longstreet alone we would have run the last one into the Tennessee River, but Bragg held us up and gave them time to "catch their breath" and stop at Chattanooga and at the base of Lookout Mountain. Here we remained for the most of the fall and here we had the hardest service of the entire war.

The rainy season came on—cold, sleet and snow—and the creeks in our rear got so swollen that we were cut off from our supplies. We had a tough time getting something to eat. So scarce were rations that some men in our regiment tore down barns catching rats, which they would boil and put in "drop dumplings" and did have good stews. Finally Col. Kilpatrick had a detail of axmen to fell trees, out of which he had a large raft made, and sent a detail across the expanse of water and brought us in meal, bacon, salt and whatever there was. Ours was the only regiment so fortunate.

While here we one afternoon received orders to prepare for a recognizance. Our brigade was taken across the base of Lookout Mountain and about dark crossed Chattanooga Creek, into Wahatchie Valley, where a heavy supply train had been discovered earlier in the day. Our object was to capture this train and bring the supplies in. After crossing Chattanooga Creek on a bridge, the only way this creek could be crossed, we were thrown into line of battle. Hampton Legion, Col. Gary, on the extreme right, Sixth South Carolina next, Fifth next, First next, Second next, with Palmetto Sharpshooters on extreme left. Capt. James Hagood's company, Company K, of Orangeburg, was deployed as skirmishers in front of our regiment. I was orderly for the colonel. We commenced the advance through these woods—underbrush, hills, hollows and holes—and kept as quiet as we could. But then we made considerable fuss.

After advancing this way for perhaps two or three miles, Hagood's skirmishers struck them in front of us. At the same time the Fifth and Sixth and the Legion struck them. It was so that the Legion got right into the train before being discovered, and they went to turning loose the mules and raising Cain in general. In front of the Fifth, First, Second and Sharpshooters there were no wagons. We had struck them but a few moments when they were ready to receive us, and lo and behold, we were in front of Hooker's army corps—one of the best corps of fighters in the entire Yankee army.

Here we were in a mess. Jenkins' brigade, composed of not more than one thousand men, confronting and attacking the strongest and best army corps in the Yankee service. In our advance we were so placed that the left of the First Regiment was resting on the railroad, the right of the Second resting on the same, the railroad between us. We advanced till our regiment got out of the woods and into a field. Fighting along the entire line was intense and heavy; we had advanced as far as we could and had lain down, continuing the heavy fighting. After being here under one of the heaviest firing I ever saw for perhaps an hour, men being killed and wounded every second, I was lying down alongside Col. Kilpatrick, who was on his knees making observations—a minnie ball struck the colonel, killing him instantly, passing through his heart.

At the very moment this occurred I heard someone call Lieut. Clowney, and he, leaving me, responded to the call. Then I saw Col. Bratton, who was that night commanding the brigade (Gen. Jenkins acting major-general) sitting on his old gray horse, smoking his old *meerschaum* pipe. He said, "Clowney, where is Kilpatrick?" Clowney informed him that he was just then killed. Col. Bratton said, "Get him off the field. We are going to fall back," and then said, "I want a man to carry some orders for me."

Lieut. Clowney called out, "Come here, Mixson." I went up to

Col. Bratton and took hold of his horse's mane; he looked down at me and said, "My little man, all the staff are either killed or wounded. I want some orders extended. Can you do it?"

I replied, "I can try, colonel."

He answered, "That is all that any of us can do. You are very small, but I can trust you. You must run across the railroad and tell Col. Bowen, of the Second, that we are falling back. The Legion, Sixth and Fifth are now moving; your regiment will fall in behind the Fifth, and the Second will fall in behind the First; and you hear that heavy firing away over yonder? That is the Sharpshooters. Find Col. Walker and tell him we are all gone—to pull off and get back on our trail and save himself the best he can. *Go, my little man.*"

I went up on the side of the railroad embankment; stopping a moment or two until a shell had passed—they were making the railroad every half minute—between shells I ran across and down the embankment and right into the arms of Col. Bowen. Just then one of those shells bursted and knocked sand over us and knocked us both down. I delivered my orders to him and started across the open field to find Col. Walker with the Sharpshooters. (You must not forget that all this was under a galling fire of musketry from 10,000 guns). I got up pretty close and stopped behind a persimmon tree; it being dark and raining, I could not see whom I was approaching—it might be Yankees—but I stopped and called out.

"What regiment is that?" and was told Palmetto Sharpshooters. Still, to make safe, I inquired, "Who is your colonel?" and was told Col. Walker. Then I ventured up and found Col. Walker, to whom I delivered the message. He made me tell him why I was carrying orders for Col. Bratton, and he was then satisfied that the orders were straight. On delivering these orders, and not realizing the length of time I had been at it, I ran back from whence I had come. I missed the Second Regiment, but took no notice of that; ran up and across the railroad embankment and down the other side. I ran into a spring about waist deep.

On pulling out of this I discovered that the regiment had gone. There being no more shelling on the railroad I took down it in the direction I knew was right. I had not gone more than two hundred yards when I ran up with two men. I asked who they were, and upon their giving me the number of a Yankee regiment I ordered them to surrender, which they did, throwing down their guns. *I had none.* I then relieved them of their haversacks, knives and whatever else they had, and then it was found out that the Yankees had advanced and we were in their rear. But with my two prisoners I continued down the railroad. We had not gone far when we were hailed from the side of the road, "Who's there?" I answered, "First South Carolina Volunteers," when a volley was fired into us. I rolled down the embankment on the opposite side and made tracks, then turned across toward where I had been to hunt the Sharpshooters. What became of my prisoners I never knew.

I finally got on the trail of the Sharpshooters, and when I struck Chattanooga Creek I found the brigade had recrossed and there were some of Company E at the bridge. They had cut the bridge away from the bank and had it on fire; this to prevent the Yankees from following us, as the creek was impassable except at the bridge. I was here again in a quandary. About ten or twelve feet of the bridge gone, the balance on fire. Darling Sprawls, of Williston, came to the end on fire and told me to take a running jump and he would try to catch me. I did so, and, as luck would have it, he caught me and pulled me in. This got me back within our lines and saved me from becoming a prisoner.

CHAPTER 6

Forage & Furlough

Our brigade, or the remnant of it, reached our quarters some time after sunrise, and then it was that we commenced to realize the loss that we had sustained during the night in the Wahatchie Valley. We had lost in killed, wounded and missing over one-half of our number, and when we got back to quarters we looked "mighty scarce" and few. I don't recollect who among the officers of our regiment were killed besides Col. Kilpatrick, but it seemed as if all the regiment were *gone*. Only a few left to tell the tale.

One of my nephews, G. D. Mixson, was missing. We did not know whether killed, wounded or captured, and many other poor fellows left behind. Col. Bratton, having no one left on his staff, sent for Jim Diamond, of Company E, and took him on as orderly for several days. Capt. Grimes, of Company G, Bamberg, being the senior officer, took command of the regiment, which left Lieut. Sweat in command of Company G. We did nothing after this escapade for some time but rest up and recruit. The winter was coming on now in earnest and cold weather and rains were upon us.

One cold night I was short of cover, and I had to have some more somehow, so I went out during the dark hours. It was not long before I ran upon a nest of four old "Rebs" sleeping soundly, warm and snug. I cautiously crept up and found that the top blanket was a heavy army blanket, large and thick; I determined to have that blanket. So, waiting a little time, quietly took the corners of the blanket at the feet, made a good strong pull, and darted into the dark, off and away, before they could realize their loss. *And the blanket was mine.* Many a night after that did that same blanket keep me warm.

Another of my nephews, B. F. Nelson, was lost to us here. He was taken sick and sent off to Newnan, Ga., to the hospital, where he died.

One night after dark our regiment was ordered to fall in, and we were carried across Peavine Creek to feel the enemy. We had to cross this creek on a fallen tree which reached from bank to bank. The banks being some eight feet above the water, and the water being deep, we literally "cooned" it over. We did not go far before we ran on the Yanks and met a warm reception. We certainly *felt them*. We remained "feeling" them for over an hour and then retired, recrossing the creek at the same place in the same manner we had crossed. In this fight we had several killed and quite a number wounded.

Among the killed was Lieut. Sweat, commanding Company G, of Bamberg, a good man and a brave officer. How they ever got him back across that creek I have never known, but he was brought back. This was the last of any happenings with and around Chattanooga. It was not long after this before we got orders to move, and we felt that we were to make our way back to Virginia. It seemed to us that we were going back home and it brought a good feeling over every man in the corps. The evening before we broke camp the band played "*Take Me Back to Old Virginia*," and Longstreet's Corps bade farewell to Bragg's Army and the West in prolonged cheers.

On leaving our camps next morning we marched a distance of eight miles to Tyner's Station, where we were loaded in freight boxes. Upon reaching the Valley of the Sweetwater we stopped about a week and got a plenty to eat, when we crossed the Tennessee River at Loudon. The weather had gotten cold, and we had a time crossing this river. This was done on a bridge made as follows:

We had a lot of boats made and these boats were secured to a chain stretched across the river and planks laid from boat to boat. It was not a very safe passage way, but we passed over without any mishaps. Capt. Foster, of the Palmetto Sharpshooters, was in command of the detail to put in this bridge. It was so cold that the ice would cover the chain from end to end and the men suffered much from cold while at this work.

Capt. Foster was from Union, S. C., and is still alive and quite wealthy, and is one of the best business men today in Union. For the next few days we had running fights with the enemy, *they doing the running*. Just before reaching Campbell Station we captured a train of eighty wagons well loaded with supplies, which they had left in their hurry. This came in mighty well, but there was not any clothing or shoes, the things we most needed just then, for we were both naked and barefooted. We expected a big fight around Campbell Station, but somehow they got away after some heavy skirmishing. While following the enemy very closely and keeping them in the continued "go-along" here we caught them one morning while they were cooking breakfast and rushed into them. They took to their heels and we got the breakfast. As we dashed into them I ran upon a fine mare tied to an oak limb with a halter. I captured her, and, taking her by the halter, continued the charge, she trotting along making the charge with me.

In a very short while Dr. J. S. Stoney, of Allendale, our assistant surgeon, dashed up to me and asked me for the mare. I had no use for her and made him a present of her, and he sent her home by Tom, his negro boy. She is the mother and grandmother of the famous four-mile racers which had such a reputation for speed and distance, owned by Dr. Stoney.

Our next place to hold up was around Knoxville, where we had some hard service and hard fighting. We invested Knoxville on all sides and had two days' fighting, driving the enemy back into their entrenchments, and on the morning of the third day we made the attack on Fort Sanders. The attack was made about sunrise, one of the coldest mornings I think I ever felt. We were in tatters, so far as clothing went, and a great many barefooted, but with the accustomed endurance of the men who had suffered from the same cause on previous occasions, we did not falter.

In making the charge on Fort Sanders we went through frozen bogs and over felled trees, trimmed up with the limbs sharpened and pointing towards us. Picking our way the best we could through this barricade, we slowly and gradually drew closer to the fort, but we struck an obstacle which we found hard to overcome. Among these felled trees there were barbed wires interlined about six inches apart, and some five feet high. Having nothing to cut the wires and no way to get through we were ordered to give up the attempt. Our loss was considerable, but not so great as might be supposed, taking into consideration the very slow advance we had made. We retired in good order, not beaten, but just failed, because there was no earthly way to do more.

We were then taken hurriedly to Rodgersville, a distance of some fifty miles, where we expected to go into winter quarters, but remained here only a few days. While here Capt. Jim Hagood, of Company K, was made colonel; Capt. B. B. Kirkland, Company C, of Buford's Bridge, lieutenant-colonel, and Capt. Grimes, of Company G, of

Bamberg, major. You see from this that Jim Hagood, who had joined Capt. Kirkland's Company, had risen from private—over his captain and the other senior officers of the regiment. Col. Hagood was only nineteen years old when he was appointed colonel. After being at Rodgersville only a few days we were carried on a forced march to McBean Station, where the enemy had nearly succeeded in getting in our rear. We again put them on the run and the army then headed for Morristown, where they went into winter quarters.

Our brigade, however, was sent out at Rodgersville on a foraging expedition to report to the army at Morristown. We were on this expedition for nearly two weeks, having all the wagons of Longstreet's corps to fill up. We had quite a good time while on this detached service, so far as eating was concerned. While the officers were doing their work in a big way, we fellows were doing ours in a much smaller way; and many a chicken, turkey, goose, pig, went into our private haversacks.

Jim Diamond, of Barnwell, was at that time a wagon driver. One night he told me to come with him next morning, that we could take a mule apiece and put in a good day; that he had seen some nice geese about four miles off and we would try for them. I went next morning and we jumped on a mule apiece, I bareback. Jim headed the way to where he knew the geese were. He was prepared himself, and before reaching the place he instructed me to follow and ask no questions. On riding up to the farm house, the old lady of the house came out to talk to us. We tried to get something to eat from her, but she wanted *money*. This country was nearly all Unionist and bushwhackers.

Having no money, we failed to outtalk her, and, as the geese were out on the front, we decided to start. Jim had a fishing line, and as we rode by the geese he baited his hook with a grain of corn and threw it down near an old gander, who immediately gobbled it up. Jim tightened on his line and found he had him hooked. We started off then in a slow trot, and as Jim commenced to pull the gander commenced to pull too. Jim held his hold and the old fellow came flopping behind with his wings outstretched, looking as if he was showing fight. The balance of the drove fell in behind the old gander, and away we went. The old woman looked on in utter amazement and cried out to us, "Don't run; he can't hurt you," but running right then was our idea, and, after getting them all down the road in a kind of a bottom, I held the line and Jim jumped down and with a stick killed six of as fine, fat geese as were ever raised.

After visiting a place or two where we *did* manage to get some meal and flour and salt, talking the people out of it, we concluded to get back—had enough for one day. We were right good with our supply, giving the men in the company four of the geese. The other two we cooked and invited Col. Hagood, Col. Kirkland, Dr. Bellinger and Capt. Wood to take supper with us. We had a big supper about 1 o'clock at night, but the lateness of the hour did not interfere with any one's appetite.

As soon as we got our wagon train all loaded we headed out for Morristown to take things into the then hungry army, and right glad were they to see us and our train all laden down. This was just before Christmas, and we had enough to put us up a good Christmas dinner, after adding to it in private foraging parties. On Christmas Eve a couple of our company went out and on returning some time during the night they brought in a bee hive wrapped up in a blanket. Next morning they knocked off the head and took out the honey. At that time the bees were cold and not much trouble, but towards the middle of the day, the sun shining brightly, they warmed up, and there was a mess. The bees took the camp and many a fellow got a good stinging.

It was announced here at our winter quarters that all those who had not been home should have a chance for a furlough—so many men to one furlough. Our regiment was entitled to only one, and there were but three who had not been home; there were myself, who had no family at home; Hughes, from Bamberg, who had a wife and children whom he had not seen since he left them in May, 1861, and one other in the same fix as Hughes. I never saw people so excited over the drawing as the other two. As for myself, I did not care much. Hughes was the most anxious man I ever saw. The papers were put in a hat, one marked "furlough," the other two blank. Hughes drew first—got a blank. The other fellow drew; he, too, got a blank, leaving the paper marked "furlough" in the hat for me.

These two good old soldiers actually cried. They could fight, march naked and barefoot, do without something to eat—all without a murmur. But being so near to getting a furlough and then to miss, it was too much. *I could not stand it.* So I told them to put two papers in the hat, one blank and one "furlough;" I would give my privilege away. This was done and these two prepared to draw. By this time everybody was excited over the event and a big crowd had gathered to see the result.

45

As Hughes had drawn first before, it was decided that the other fellow should do so this time. He put his hand forward to go into the hat. His hand was shaking and he was excited to death. Hughes, poor fellow, stood looking on. He was a pitiful sight. He could hardly stand up—his legs were shaking. Despair was depicted on his face. The hand already forward went down into the hat and slowly out it came. I believe both men had their eyes shut. Someone read, "furlough." *Hughes had again lost.* It was pitiful to see him, but the other fellow was happy. It was strange that Hughes never did get home till after the surrender.

CHAPTER 7

A Brief Respite

We are now in winter quarters near Morristown in the coldest country and the wettest country I ever saw. Fortunately, we have tents plenty, wood abundant and a good country to get something to eat. It is too cold and wet to drill, therefore, we have nothing to do but rest up, patch our old clothes as best we can, and our barefoot boys resort to the method of tying up their feet in pieces of blankets, making a kind of moccasin. Were we properly clothed and shod we would be comparatively comfortable. This East Tennessee country is a fine country for hogs, cattle, eggs, chickens, flour, meal, bee-gums and maple syrup. We are certainly on the go, hunting and finding some of all these things, but as I am one of those who are totally without a covering to my feet and my breeches are too far gone to even take a patch, I cannot get out much.

But Jim Diamond is as good as ever hunting up these things, and our mess has a plenty to eat. He even sometimes comes in with a little applejack, and then we have a "jollification" sure enough. Col. Hagood and Capt. Wood have about joined our mess for good. They having a negro boy cook, each one generally goes out with Jim, while the other remains and cooks, and the colonel and captain have some money—we have none. We could not very well refuse to take them in with us.

We had not been here more than three weeks when we heard some fighting going on down on Strawberry Plains, thirteen miles off. Our cavalry had run up on a lot of moving Yankee infantry and had attacked them. We were called out and formed line of march. This was bitter cold weather and this was a hard march on us, especially those of us who were barefoot, among whom I was one. We barefoot fellows wrapped up our feet the best we could and fell in with the balance.

The woods were full of water from the rains and were so hard frozen that the ice did not break with the weight of the horses.

We hurriedly arrived near the fighting, and, just on the edge of the plain in which the fight was going on, and in a thick woods, all the barefoot men were ordered to fall out and make fires. It was only a short way to the firing, and, instead of "falling out," I had an eye for the future. We went into the open fields in a double quick line of battle. The enemy fell back as we advanced. We had not gone more than a couple of hundred yards before we ran over some dead Yankees. Here was my opportunity, and I embraced it. The first one I got to I stopped, pulled off his pants, shoes and stockings, got right into them, there and then. The shoes were new and fit perfectly; the stockings were good wool and came up to my knees, and the pants were all right, except a little too long, but I rolled them up about as they are worn these days and they, too, were a fit. I felt *grand*.

The fight was soon over, with no casualties on our side. We then started for our return trip and I felt very sorry for those poor barefoot devils who took the opportunity of stopping at a fire rather than go a little further and have the chance of "rigging out" in a good outfit. They had to take it back as they had come.

A few days after this a lady came into our camp and asked Col. Hagood for a guard to protect her place, saying she would feed us and sleep us. I was sent in charge of the detail. Along with me was Jimmie Brabham, a son of Maj. J. J. Brabham, of Buford's Bridge. Maj. Brabham was, after the war, Clerk of the Court of Barnwell County for a good many years and was the first captain of Company C while around Charleston and the islands the first year of the war. We were sent out (Jim Brabham and myself) with the lady, who took us to her home about four miles from our camp. We were all afoot. When we got to her home we discovered that we were outside of our lines, about equi-distant between our lines and the Yankee lines, perhaps a mile from each.

When I discovered this I determined to go back and give up the scheme, but the lady told me that she was Mrs. McDonald, the wife of a Yankee major, who was encamped not more than three miles off. It was he who sent her for a guard, and he told her to pledge our protection from the Yankees. Jim and I concluded to stay, and Mrs. McDonald assigned us to a nice, warm room, good feather bed with plenty of warm covering. We remained here with her and her two children, a boy of about thirteen years and a girl, named Becky, about sixteen years, for thirty-eight days.

Mrs. McDonald was very kind to us. We had the biggest kind of oak fires in the sitting room all day, and the fires would be there through the entire night. We would go to bed usually at about ten o'clock. Only about two nights in the week Mrs. McDonald would say, "Go to bed earlier tonight, boys, the major is coming." He used to come home about two nights a week, but we never got to see him, nor did we care to see him. Mrs. McDonald was a good cook, along with everything else, and she surely did feed us well on the best— principally sausages and big hominy. Jim and I would go up on the side of the mountains with the little boy, his mule and slide, and help haul wood which was already cut.

On one occasion Mrs. McDonald asked me to go to mill for her; the meal was out. She had the corn shelled, and told me the mill was inside the Yankee lines, but the major had told the picket on duty at the mill not to molest me. Well, I decided that as they had been true to us in everything else, when they could have taken us any night, that there was no danger. So Jim helped me to get about three bushels of corn up on the mule, gave me "a leg," and then, getting direction, I pulled out for the mill. I found the mill at least two miles, or it seemed to me. As I rode on the end of the mill dam some half dozen Yankees came out of the mill house, all well armed. I could not but feel a little uneasy, but when I reached the house they bid me, "Good morning, Johnny." They helped me off and took in the sack of corn. We sat around in the sunshine and talked till the corn was ready, when they put it up on the mule and helped me up and bade me goodbye.

Near Mrs. McDonald's home were several other homes, and nearly every night we would have company in the persons of some young ladies who would spend the evenings, sometimes remaining till eleven or twelve o'clock. They would jump on poor Jim and me and give us the devil in a friendly way. They seemed to like us very much. I remember they had a song which they would sing us, something like this:

Some near day you will hear the Yankees say,
To old Jeff Davis, 'You had better get away,
For we will raise the Union band,
Make the Rebels understand,
To leave our land
Or submit to Abraham.'

They would have a jolly time with us and we equally as jolly a time with them. To show how well the major took care of us from his people, we would even go home with the girls all hours of the night and were never disturbed. But this could not last forever, and the time came when we were called in; and two days after we struck camp and started again for Virginia. On passing through Morristown I saw Mrs. McDonald, Becky and Tom and several of the young ladies who had been to visit us at the McDonalds, on a street corner. They had gone to town to see us off and bade us goodbye. They called us out of ranks and seemed real sorry to see us go. I have often thought of the good people and wondered if the major got through all right. I hope he did.

We kept on the move until we reached Bristol, Tenn., when we stopped a couple of days to rest up. After which we moved again and stopped a day or two at Chancellorsville, and then on to Gordonsville, where we were met by Gen. Lee and had a grand review by the grand old chieftain, who seemed as happy to have us back as we were to get back. Gen. Lee must have felt good in getting the welcome extended him by those who had been lost to him so long. The men hung around him and seemed satisfied to lay their hands on his gray horse or to touch the bridle, or the stirrup, or the old general's leg— anything that Lee had was sacred to us fellows who had just come back. *And the general.* He could not help from breaking down. Here were men who had gone forward at his command, knowing that they might never get out; here were men who had never murmured when Lee said, "Go!" or "Come." Here were men who had suffered privation, hunger, cold, *death itself*, whenever ordered by him. He could not help giving way, and tears traced down his cheeks, and he felt that we were again to do his bidding.

We stopped over here for several days and got a good many recruits, some sick and wounded returning to us, and some other men and boys, new men who had never yet seen service. Among these were old men—Walton Hair, Mathias Hair, from Elko; John William Canady, from Tinker Creek; W. F. Kitchen, Darios Ogden and Artist Woodward, from Williston, and Eddie Bellinger, from Barnwell, and Job Rountree, from Joyce's Branch—all these for Company E, Eddie Bellinger being the only young man, and he a mere youth. These new recruits, with some sick and wounded returning, made us a right respectable company once more. We needed another officer in our company, having only Capt. Wood and Lieut. Dick Best, from Allendale, so we held an election for lieutenant, and J. Marshall Hair, of Williston, was elected.

After remaining here for perhaps two weeks, on the morning of the third day of May we took up our line of march and on the night of the fifth of May we stopped for the night within six miles of the Wilderness, having tramped sixty-odd miles in the two and a half days. When we stopped for the night we were pretty badly jaded and needed the night's rest. We had been hearing the musketry and cannonading nearly the entire day. This was kept up all night and we knew that we would be into the thickest of it early next morning, and, sure enough, we were put on the move just before day. We moved at a double quick and kept up the double quick for the entire six miles, when we reached the Wilderness and went directly into it.

CHAPTER 8

The Wilderness

We struck the plank road at the Wilderness in a double quick just after sunrise and took down it towards the battle which had been going on furiously since just after midnight. Our regiment was on the extreme left of our brigade, which placed us in rear when marching in columns of four. Our company, Company E, was on the left of the regiment, this making our company the extreme left of Jenkins' brigade. Just in rear of us was Bennings' Georgians, and the old general was on his gray horse in that slow gallop at the head of his brigade. Our division (Fields' division) was composed now of Hood's Texas Brigade, in front, Anderson's Georgia Brigade (Tige Anderson), Robertson's Alabama Brigade, Jenkins' South Carolina Brigade and Bennings' Georgia Brigade (Rock Benning). The names of Tige Anderson and Rock Benning had been given these two brigadiers a long time back.

Hood, Anderson and Robertson had reached the Wilderness earlier in the morning, some two hours ahead of Jenkins and Benning, and were heavily engaged. When we struck the plank road we were still in a double quick. We were ordered to load at the double quick. Gen. Benning was just about twenty feet in my rear. Very soon we commenced to meet the wounded coming out. These wounded fellows would step one side, giving us the right of way, and also giving words of encouragement. I noticed one old fellow using his gun for a crutch, he being shot in the leg. As we got to him he stepped out to one side, and, standing still as Gen. Benning got to him, he cried out in a loud, cheerful voice, "Go it, Rock. Tige's treed." And I guess the old fellow was telling the truth.

Benning's brigade was filed to the left of the plank road; our brigade was filed to the right of it with our left resting on the road. Just as we had cleared enough to give us room the command was given, "Left flank." This threw us in line of battle. We were ordered to halt in this position. We had hardly stopped when Kershaw's Brigade came tilting back, closely followed by the enemy. No one seemed to know that we were there, when Kershaw's men discovered us by running into us. They were happy and rallied of their own accord, and the way we did put it to those Yankees! It would have done you good to see.

We drove them easily back, as they were so surprised, but we did not follow them up but a short distance, when we stopped behind a kind of breastworks made from a few old pines piled together. Here we remained till midday under a heavy fire, and doing the same for them. During the time we were here I asked permission of Col. Hagood to let me crawl out in front and see if I couldn't get something off of the dead Yankees lying just away from us. He said it was mighty risky, but if I chose to take chances and would not go far, to go ahead. I lay flat on my belly and crawled up to the first one, then to the second, until I had visited eight of these fellows. I was always very careful to keep them between me and the Yankees. I thought I had gone far enough after getting to the eighth, so I turned back and crawled into our lines.

When I got back Jim Hagood said, "What have you got?" We were lying down, as we could not put up our heads on account of the bullets. I unloaded my pockets, turning them out on the ground. I had six watches, three or four knives, some rations and a few other trinkets. Col. Hagood took his choice of the watches and I gave Capt. Wood another. The other I sold to Sid Key, now of Beaufort, who had some Confederate money. We were still lying here in a heavy fire when, just after midday, Gen. Jenkins rode down the line in our rear. He had been hit by a bullet, breaking his little finger. He was holding out his hand, from which the blood was still trickling. He said to us, "Men of the First, we are going to charge. Now, I want each and every one of you to remember that you are South Carolinians. Remember your wives, your sweethearts, your sisters at home. Remember your duty. Col. Hagood, get your regiment ready."

Col. Hagood, the boy colonel, called out, "First regiment, continue to lie down, but be at attention." Only a few moments more and the voice of Col. Hagood was heard, "First Regiment, forward." He was the first to be up and ready to move. We crossed over our logs and then the command, "Charge!" We made a dart, and so did the Yankees, but they darted back. We followed them, running them into their works, where they had heavy reinforcements. We followed them to within some one hundred yards of these entrenchments and could go no further. Here we remained for perhaps an hour, when we leisurely fell back to our former position.

While out there in front of the Yankee works we were subjected to the most deadly fire. I had picked up a little oak stump about the size of my thigh, which had rotted off even with the ground and so badly worm eaten that I could see holes all through it. This I had stood up, propping it with a stick. I got in behind it and soon my brother Joyce moved up on my left and then Lieut. Hair came up on my right. I was square in behind the stump and now I had a man on each side. I was pretty well protected, or at least I felt so. Lieut. Hair, being on my right, turned his head to the left to talk to me. We were all lying flat on our bellies.

As he turned to speak to me a minnie ball hit him in the right temple, passing directly through his face and head, coming out in the left cheek. His head fell flat to the ground. I put my hand under his head, holding it up. The blood gushed from his temple, his eyes, his nose, his mouth. I held him thus until the blood in a manner stopped, then taking his handkerchief I wiped his eyes and asked him if he could get back. He thought he could, and, on standing up, a minnie ball cut his tobacco pouch from his coat. However, he started back, and after running for perhaps a hundred yards I saw him almost turn a somersault. I thought then he was a "goner," but he is yet alive, (as at time of first publication), living at Williston, and making a good, upright, intelligent citizen.

On getting back from where we had made the charge we were soon moved to the left. This time we were supporting a brigade in Pickett's Division, marching in line of battle some forty yards in rear of their line of battle. I think I have failed to mention that the entire Wilderness was one mass of undergrowth—oaks from about the size of one's finger to the size of one's wrist, and about as tall as a tall man's head. The section of the woods we were now advancing into was remarkably thicker than any we had yet encountered, and, worse still, it seemed as if everyone had a bullet through it from the hard fighting that had just gone on there, causing these white oak runners to bend down from being top heavy. These bullets all seemed to go through about the height of a man's waist. In tumbling down they made almost an impassable barrier.

Together with this obstacle the dead and dying were so thick that we could not help stepping on them. It has been said that a person could walk seven miles, stepping from body to body, and never touch the ground.

We were supporting the Virginians. They neared the plank road, marching parallel thereto, the Yankees falling back. As they got very near the road they saw a Yankee flag waving just above the bushes and just about the road. It was natural to suppose that the enemy had halted and was making a stand on this road. They immediately opened fire. The flag fell, and, as there was no response, we discovered that Longstreet, Jenkins and their staffs had ridden down this road, thinking we had crossed. Longstreet, seeing a Yankee flag lying on the road, had ordered one of his staff to pick it up. This he did, and, remounting, the flag was raised above the bushes and became unfurled. The Virginians fired on it, killing Gen. Jenkins and dangerously wounding Longstreet and some of their staff. This was a great misfortune to us. Here fell two of our best officers. It was a long time before Longstreet was well enough to return to us, but he did after a while; but was ever after suffering with his left side and shoulder.

While we were halted here in the confusion after happening to this misfortune, I ran upon a dead Yankee officer, finely dressed, clean and nice looking. He had on a fine pair of high top boots, brand new, the spurs, of course, coming with them. I immediately took them to Col. Hagood and he found them as good a fit as if made for him. We ran the enemy back to their entrenchments on this part of the line as we had done in the morning on the other part. We then fell back far enough to be out of range of their musketry, and without even taking off our cartridge boxes—no fires—we lay down to rest and get some sleep.

We did not sleep much this night, for we were right in among the dead and dying, and many a poor fellow, especially from the Yankee army, would beg for water, and we did not have it to give him. Our men got some canteens from the dead, some with a little water and some with brandy. All this was given to the poor fellows without any regard to which side he belonged. All we cared for was that he was a human being and a brother, though we had fought him hard all day.

Remaining here for the night, with only a little firing on the skirmish line, we retired some short distance next morning; only far enough back to get off of the ground where there were so many dead. Here we remained all day of the seventh and that night until about four or five o'clock on the morning of the eighth, when we were moved to our right. Grant had started his flank movement for Richmond by trying to turn our left. We met him on the eighth at Spotsylvania and here again we had a most bloody battle.

CHAPTER 9

Spotsylvania

On May 7th, the day after the big fight at the Wilderness, we moved back a short distance and got off of the field, where it was strewn with the dead and dying. Here we remained sharpshooting heavily all day; but about dark that held up and we were comparatively quiet. We cooked our suppers and prepared for a good night's sleep and a much needed rest, as we had been hard at it for over forty-eight hours. It was not long after dark before all of us were fast asleep, except those on picket. Grant, however, had other views than to rest. He was just starting on his "On to Richmond."

As the hours grew on, the skirmishing grew less, but yet there was commotion in the enemy's lines. Near midnight we were ordered in line and moved off—*the whole of Lee's army*. We were moved to our right, for Grant was moving on Richmond by the left. We met them after a hard march, hard only because we were so broken down. At Spotsylvania, shortly after midday, and without having time to rest or even catch our breath, we met them—*we had to stop them*. Our brigade was thrown in front of a lot of Pennsylvanians, who seemed to think no one had the right to stop them from going right on to Richmond. But it did not take us more than a couple of hours that evening to convince them this was not the day nor time to go undisputed. In little less than two hours they had fallen back, leaving us where we met them.

The Palmetto Sharpshooters of our brigade captured here a regiment of Pennsylvanians, over four hundred men. We did not follow them, I suppose because we were too tired and broken down to run when we met them, and were the same way and could not follow. It was now almost sundown, and, after sending out our skirmishers, we began to look around to see how the land lay; for we expected hard fighting again after what we had at the Wilderness.

The men, of their own accord, commenced to cut down pine trees to build breastworks. The only tools we had for this purpose were the little hand axes, about three inches wide, which some of the men had. These they had carried in their belts and used them to chop wood for fires. But now they put them to bigger use and would not hesitate to jump onto a pine tree that would square twenty inches; and it was surprising how soon they would have it down, cut off, trimmed up and cut off again. Then the whole company would take it up, place it in position. We worked this way for some hours into the night. All the while the whole skirmish line was pretty warmly engaged.

That was a great incentive to us, and we worked until we had to quit because we were just broken down. But we had put up some log work which would be a great protection before we did quit. We got a very good night's sleep, and next morning, after eating what little we had, we felt real good and ready to go to work again on our breastworks. This we did, and while our skirmish line was fighting in our front and the hard fight going on "at the angle" on our right, we worked. And by afternoon we had a set of breastworks of which we were proud. The Yankees did not attack our part of the line during the day—only kept our pickets heavily engaged.

Now, this night was Company E's time for picket, and before dark we were carried out to the line, relieving the company already there. Our company had at this time sixteen men, all told, and we had to cover the entire front of the whole regiment. Consequently, we were not at regulation distance apart when we deployed as skirmishers. We, however, relieved the other company and fell in behind a rail fence. We expected an advance at any moment. Our orders were to hold the ground as long as we could. After dark three of us rallied together and remained so. This made some distance from one squad to another, but it was the best we could do. Where each three men were we "let the fence down," making a jam, and then, getting in this, we had right good protection. There were in one jam Eddie Bellinger, Job Rountree and myself.

Well, at midnight they advanced, and it was hot for some time. Eddie Bellinger and myself could load our guns lying down on our backs, but Job could not do it. He was used to hunting squirrels around Mixson's Mill Pond and Joyce's Branch and had never had to lie down to load. He thereupon proposed to Eddie and me that if we would do the loading he would do the shooting. This we readily agreed to, and

Job would stand up, exposing himself from waist up. As soon as we would get a gun loaded we would pass it to him, and he would throw the empty gun back for another loaded one. We had three guns and worked them so fast that they got so hot we stopped loading for fear they would not stand it.

We finally drove this advance back, after an hour's hard work. We were not disturbed any more till morning. Just as the sun began to show itself we discovered a line of battle advancing over the hill, where they had come a little nearer. There was another supporting the first and then yet another supporting the second, making an advance of three lines of battle. We knew we were in for it now, sure, and we poor little sixteen men opened on them just the same as if we were an army.

But on they came, as if we were not there. It reminded me of the gnat on the bull's horn. On they came, and soon we heard Capt. Wood say, "Skirmishers, fall back, firing." We went back, going from tree to tree. They were gaining on us, as we were retiring slowly. The last stand we made was some seventy-five yards in front of our breastworks. We stopped here and gave them a round or two. We were protected by trees. My brother Joyce and myself happened to stop in behind the same tree. We both shot off our guns and reloaded. When he went to cap his gun he let the cap slip through his fingers, and, instead of reaching in his cap box for another, he stooped over to pick it up from the ground, thereby exposing a part of his person. *No sooner exposed than hit*, and he made for the works.

Just then Capt. Wood gave command, "Skirmishers, into the works," and in we went. We were glad, too, when we got behind them. By this time, or by the time we had assembled as a company and taken our company's position in the regiment, the enemy's three lines had gotten up pretty close. The front line had advanced to within about forty yards of our works and had lain down. The second line was some twenty yards in the rear of these, and the third line about the same distance in rear of the second. All three lines were now lying down. We were well protected behind the good breastworks of logs, and the way we did give it to those Yankees would have done your heart good to see; and they—well, they stood it like men, but it was too much for them to go forward, and, after staying there for perhaps an hour, they fell back; but not for long.

They came again, and about the same thing happened the second time, after they had again remained for nearly an hour. Again they fled back, but in a short time back they came, seemingly with more vim than ever, and at one time it seemed that they would run over us. But we held on, and, showing no indication of giving way, they got no further than the works, which they did reach, but could not climb over. Here it was hot for a few moments, but they weakened, and for the third time fell back; but this time some two hundred yards, when they rallied. They were, however, somewhat demoralised and Col. Hagood, noticing this, and taking advantage of it, hollered out, "Company E, deploy as skirmishers."

While we were deploying behind the works Col. Hagood passed an order that when the skirmishers started to advance the whole regiment must yell as we mounted the works. Then the command was given, "Skirmishers, forward, double quick." At this time there were not more than ten or twelve men in the skirmish line charging three lines of battle. As we mounted the works the regiment gave the yell. The whole of Lee's army, both to the right and left, seemed to take it up, and on we went, *this handful*. The Yankees must have thought our whole army was out after them, for they broke in confusion. It was really rich to see ten or twelve men running as many thousands.

In making this advance I ran over a nice looking fellow who was just dead. I happened to notice a gold ring on his finger, and as the enemy were getting back as fast as they could, I concluded to get that ring. So, stooping over, I pulled it off, and upon straightening up I saw a body of Yankees at right shoulder shift and at a double quick, an officer with drawn sword in command, coming up on our left, *now in our rear*. I called out to Capt. Wood, "They are flanking us on the left, captain." He stopped and looked and gave the command, "Skirmishers, in retreat." He and I started back, and to get back we had to pass just at the head of these Yankees.

As we got at their head the officer in command of them ordered his men to halt, and, turning his sword, tendered it to Capt. Wood, thereby surrendering the lot. Capt. Wood immediately cried out, "Skirmishers, halt, forward. Frank, take charge of these men." I stepped up, gave the command, "File right, double quick," and in no time the whole lot were in our works, thirty-six prisoners. It seems that we had been fighting all day fresh troops from Vermont, and the unexpected advance of our skirmish line led this entire company to believe that they were behind our advancing columns.

It had been raining all day, and we were as black with powder as the negroes at home. Our hands and faces would get wet, and taking our cartridges out and biting off the stem we would get the powder on our hands and faces.

It was now late in the afternoon and another company was sent to relieve us. We had been on the skirmish line since the evening before. On passing back to our works I stopped and foraged a little; and when I went into our works I was literally loaded down with haversacks, knapsacks and hats. I had six Stetson hats—new—and, on opening the knapsacks the things which struck my fancy most were white laundered shirts (boiled shirts). I gave a hat to Col. Hagood, Capt. Wood, Lieut. Dick Bryan, Lieut. Dick Best, Jim Diamond, and kept one myself. The dry goods and rations were divided out to the company. It was amusing to see us with our faces as black as chimney sweeps with a white starched shirt on. We got our supper all right that night and slept like logs. The firing on the picket line did not worry us enough to keep us awake, though at times it seemed as if they were coming again. This ended the third day at Spotsylvania.

CHAPTER 10

The Mighty Few

We had a comparatively quiet night after this hard day's work and slept pretty well, lying down in ranks behind our breastworks. The rain that had been falling the entire day ceased during the early part of the night. We did not make down our beds, nor even take off our accoutrements; but then we had not done that since the night before the Wilderness. Next morning, after we had prepared and eaten our breakfast, the little we had, we were relieved by some other troops, and we were taken up on the right in and about the Angle; but just as we got there our troops had made an assault and had gained what they had lost. Therefore, we were not actively in the engagement, though we were in it enough to be under a heavy fire, and we had some men both killed and wounded. I recollect that Lieut. Dick Steedly, of Company G, Bamberg, who was commanding that company, was wounded while we were on this part of the line, and others, too, whom I cannot recall.

We remained on this part of the line during the day, being kept in readiness to go to any point where we might be needed. We were kept close up to the fighting line, and, while not being engaged, yet we were close enough and were under a heavy fire during the entire day. We must have remained at this position that night. Next morning the enemy seemed to have moved down to their right—our left—and the fighting was heavy there. We were hurried down to that part of the line. We found a heavy fight going on, but the Georgians, whom we went to support, were holding their own, and we were held back ready to support any part that might give way. The Georgians finally made an assault and drove the enemy back and followed them closely for some distance. While this was going on we were lining quickly in rear, ready to move in any direction.

While waiting here Eddie Bellinger and I concluded to "nose around" and see if we could run on to anything. Rations were now scarce, and something to eat would go good. Without saying a word to anyone except Jim Diamond, we walked off in the direction of the front, where the Georgians were now skirmishing. We soon reached their line and passed on through to the front. The skirmishing had about this time ceased. We continued to go on to the front and pass the skirmish line. The battlefield of the days before was just ahead of us, and we knew if we could get to where the dead were we would get something sure.

Cautiously now, for we were in advance of our pickets and knew nothing of the whereabouts of the Yankees. But for something to eat we were taking chances. We at last came upon the ground where the dead of several days were lying. We had not searched but a few when heavy firing began on the right, and we discovered the pickets from outside advancing. Immediately there was a perfect fusillade on the picket line on the right. We knew it would extend to where we were and catch us between the lines.

Consequently, we determined to get "away back." We started back in a hurry, and when the Georgia picket line saw us coming back as hard as we could run they thought the Yankees were right in behind us, and they broke. The captain in command of the pickets soon discovered that the enemy were not making an advance, that Eddie and I had caused the whole confusion. He rallied his picket line, and by that time we were up with them. The old man was mad at us and he gave us the hardest "cussing" you ever heard; but we kept right on back and were soon with our company. We had three or four haversacks pretty well filled, and it was not long before Jim Diamond had a fire and had on it in tin cans sliced bacon and rice, making a pillau.

It must have smelt good, for it was not long before Gen. Bratton and Col. Simms, his adjutant-general, came up near where we were cooking. Then Col. Hagood, Adjt. Clowney, Capt. Wood, all gathered near. In due course of time Jim took off his cans, some half dozen quarts, set them around, flattened out some pine paddles and invited up the gang. Did they come? You should have seen how readily they accepted the invitation. Not one of them hesitated in the least, and the best part was that there was just about enough for all. You should have seen that crowd after the feast, getting out their pipes, filling up and lolling back, seemingly perfectly contented.

While upon the field of battle I came upon one poor fellow with his head completely gone, taken off even with his shoulders, evidently by a cannon ball. In taking his watch from his waist-band pocket, I felt a small roll of something. On investigating I found a few greenback bills sewed up in his waist-band. There were two tens and a five. As soon as Sid Key knew I had them he was after a trade, and I finally sold to him for three hundred and seventy-five Confederate.

The fighting had now about ceased along the entire line, except sharpshooting, which was kept up pretty regularly and rapidly enough to keep us expecting something at any time. But as the evening wore on nothing more serious occurred. I guess that we must have remained at this point during the night—I cannot recollect—but I think next morning all sharpshooting had stopped and everything on the entire line seemed to be perfectly quiet. During the morning we were moved, and we soon discovered that we were off again to meet Grant somewhere else, as he failed to get through at Spotsylvania, as well as the Wilderness, and was again moving to his left, still on his way to Richmond.

We held up that night in the vicinity of Hanover Junction, where we confronted the enemy. We remained here, I think, three days, with the enemy in front and heavy skirmishing and sharpshooting going on, but no regular engagement was had here. They made no general advance. I guess they were about as tired and broken down as we were; and then, perhaps, Grant was holding up here for more men, as his losses at the Wilderness and Spotsylvania had been fearful. At any rate, we confronted him here for the three days, and we, too, rested up. While here one evening Col. Hagood had the regiment formed and had such orders as these read:

> For meritorious conduct, the colonel commanding takes pleasure in announcing the following promotions and appointments: Adjt. S. B. Clowney, to be captain of Company —— (I forget whether Company B or Company K); Sergt.-Major O. D. A. Wilson, to be adjutant; Private E. W. Bellinger, Company E, to be ensign, with rank of first lieutenant; Private W. R. Brabham, of Company C, to be sergeant-major; Private F. M. Mixson to be sergeant, Company E, and Private R. C. Kirkland to be corporal of Company C. They will be obeyed and respected accordingly. By order of the colonel commanding.

I think I have failed to mention that Darling Patterson, who had been our colour bearer since the Second Manassas, and had been home for some time suffering with a wound, had recovered sufficiently to return. He had, however, applied for a transfer to Hart's Battery, but this was refused until the Battery offered us two men for him, when the change was accepted. But up to this place, the two men (named Morrison and Stewart) had not reported to us, though they should have done so, and did so a short time thereafter, I think about the time we reached Petersburg.

After lying around Hanover Junction for about three days, and Grant had satisfied himself that we were there in his front, he (Grant) moved suddenly to Cold Harbor; and we moved as suddenly, and he again found us in his front. We went to Cold Harbor in a hurried march. As we were going down the public road, woods on the right and a large field on the left, we passed Keitt's South Carolina Regiment, just from the coast, drawn up in line of battle on the side of the road, we passing just in front of them. They were a fine body of men, the regiment bearing thirteen hundred strong—about twice as big as our entire brigade. They inquired of us, "What regiment are you?" and on being told the First South Carolina, they jokingly said, "This must be only one company of it." But, poor fellows, they soon learned how fast members could diminish.

We moved on down the line to our right and soon we heard the battle open in front of Keitt; and they were in it for the first time. Many a poor fellow who had so short a time left his home State in high spirits and "spoiling" for a fight on this field "bit the dust," but well did they hold their own and made several most gallant charges, not knowing what fear was. They did nobly and held their part of the line manfully. We went on down the line, and it was not long before we, too, were in it. We must have run upon the Yankees quite suddenly, for, while marching in columns of fours at a double quick, and passing into a large field through a double gate, we "filed right," and upon getting distance enough we left flanked, throwing us into line of battle and immediately charged.

I think this meeting was unexpected by both sides, because, as we double quicked through the gate, the brigade band was stationed there and was playing a lively air—perhaps "*Bonnie Blue Flag*." I know that was the only time we ever went into a fight with music, and it had the effect of putting us right into it thick and heavy before we even realized the enemy were near. It took us but a short time to break their lines and have them falling back. We had been resting for a few days and felt like fresh troops. We did not follow them up, I suppose for the reason we were acting on the defence, disputing their right to go to Richmond and holding them back.

We had no other engagement in our front. The hard fighting here was in front of Keitt. The Yankees must have known they were fresh from the coast and concentrated all their energies against them. At any rate, by night all the hard fighting was over, Grant was again repulsed, and we all remained on our respective fields. The skirmishing and sharpshooting, however, was heavy during the night and all next day, but no more advancing was done by the Yankees. We were content with holding our ground.

We remained around here for, I think, two days longer with nothing doing. I guess after these failures to break through our lines, Grant had decided to make a big circle and had pulled out, and Lee was holding us till he had located him, when he could again be in his front. The next place we met him was at Petersburg, but when he got there Lee and his handful were *still in his front*. The "On to Richmond" was started on the 5th of May at the Wilderness, and, with fighting every day and every night, on the 12th of June we confronted and held them out of Petersburg.

I think that in Longstreet's *History of the War*, in telling of this great march of Grant's and Lee's skilful manoeuvring which met and foiled him in some of the greatest and biggest battles that had ever been fought in any war, Longstreet gives Grant's army at the Wilderness at one hundred and fifty-six thousand men, with the *world* to draw from; Lee at the Wilderness with only fifty-eight thousand, you might say, regular "rag-a-muffins," in so far as something to eat, clothing, ammunition and other supplies, and nowhere on God's green earth to draw men, material or supplies; but yet when Lee confronted Grant at Petersburg we were as indomitable as the first day at the Wilderness and loved Lee more. He was certainly now the idol of his men. Longstreet says that Grant's loss from the Wilderness to Petersburg in killed and wounded was fifty-eight thousand men, the number Lee had in his entire army. So, you see, on an average, each man in Lee's army had hit his man. Besides, our losses were heavy and we confronted Grant with only a mighty few.

CHAPTER 11

Petersburg

It is strange that I cannot recall anything from Cold Harbor to Petersburg. I don't recollect when we left Cold Harbor nor how fast we were hurried, nor the distance. The first thing coming to my remembrance is reaching Petersburg. I have consulted with Capt. Foster and several others, privates like myself, of this place (Union, S. C.), who were members of the Palmetto Sharpshooters, a regiment of our brigade, and, to my surprise, they, too, are about as much in the dark as to that period as I am. I account for it this way: We had been around Cold Harbor for several days, the first two days of which we had hard fighting. The balance of the time remaining there we had only some skirmishing on the picket lines and resting up. Therefore, there were no impressions left. Besides, we needed this rest and quiet sorely, after the hard times we had undergone since the first morning at the Wilderness.

Some time passed, and, consequently, we took things easy, regardless of everything. I do not remember, nor could I find out, how we reached Petersburg. I do not think, nor can I believe, that we passed through Richmond. If not, we must have crossed the James River on pontoons below Richmond, but, be that as it may, we did reach Petersburg, and none too soon. There was a heavy fight in progress. It was then about sundown. We were thrown into line of battle and ordered to double quick.

We had gone perhaps half a mile, drawing nearer and nearer the fighting forces, when suddenly we met our men being driven back. I understand that these were Gen. Beauregard's troops, who had been holding the enemy in check all day, and had just commenced to retire, being worn out and overpowered. They immediately fell in with us, and here we checked the advancing enemy and held our line, and upon this line so held we built the famous Petersburg breastworks, such works as were never built before, and which were occupied by our troops for nine *long*, *tiresome* and *eventful* months. It is true that at first these works here were only a crude affair, we not expecting to remain in them many days; but time went on and each day saw more work done, more facilities for moving around and for living, until we had built so that we could get around—cook, eat, sleep, the same as on the level, and with comparative safety, though the least exposure of the person would guarantee a quick shot from the enemy's sharpshooters with globe-sighted guns, and they got to be such expert marksmen that they rarely ever missed.

At this time our lines were some distance apart—far enough, in fact, for us and them to keep out our pickets, and the fighting for a while was done by the picket line, the army itself being hard at work with pick and spade. The work was hard and heavy and those who would go into the trenches at night would work the time while there and be relieved by fresh troops the following night. This was done until we had good works, and until Grant had so lengthened his line that nearly all of Lee's army was required to face him, leaving but a handful to relieve those who had worked the hardest, and who were also held as a kind of reserve, ready to go to any point, should the enemy make an assault. These held in reserve would be one day one command, the next day another.

Grant now had Petersburg invested and had moved his lines up so close that we nor they had space for pickets—in fact, our videttes did not leave our works. I don't think it could have been over two hundred yards from our works to theirs. It might have been more and it might have been less. It was a long time ago and I might not recall the distance correctly; but I do recollect that it was very uncomfortably close.

About this time the two men, Morrison and Stewart, whom were given us by Hart's Battery in exchange for Darling Patterson, came to us. I must take time to give a brief description of these two men. Morrison was a great big fellow, heavy frame, about forty-five or fifty years old, heavy gray beard, and he was a real good-hearted fellow, but the report of a gun would scare him out of his breeches. He was certainly constitutionally a coward, and I really think he hated it, and when not under fire and not scared he would determine to try to not get so next time; but his good intentions would go to the wind just as soon as the bullets began to come.

The other fellow, Stewart, was a medium sized, dark complex- ioned, swarthy man, about thirty or thirty-five. He was a genuine coward and would not try, nor did he care to overcome it, but would skulk on all occasions; and, worse still, he pretended to be a preacher, and often, in the very nick of time, old Stewart would sing out, "Let's all join in prayer." He played this off on us for a little while, and would succeed in being left; but, after a while, we found him out, and would break up his little scheme, although I don't recollect his having even been gotten into a regular "sit-to" fight. About this time we got an- other recruit—one that must be mentioned in these memoirs, because I knew him before he came, and, besides, he was known to everyone from Barnwell.

John Lambert, of Barnwell, was our other new man, and why he should have selected our regiment for his service I could never un- derstand, unless it was that he had known from infancy Col. Hagood, Eddie Bellinger, Jim Diamond, Perry Manville, the Mixson boys and Nelson boys, and perhaps some others; and as he had to go some- where it was just as well to go where he knew people. Now, while John didn't love fighting, and always said that the Lord intended him to take care of himself, and he didn't purpose to disappoint the Lord, he was a jolly fellow and kept things lively with his jokes and quaint sayings. But, while he was very careful how he exposed himself, he did an act while in the trenches which the bravest of the brave shuddered at. After a time in the trenches it had gotten so that the least exposure was certain death.

One day there came along in the field in rear of our regiment a nice, fat shoat, about fifty pounds, strolling as if he didn't care if corn was fifty dollars a bushel. He strolled along till a Yankee sharpshooter concluded to cut him down. We heard him squeal and saw the shoat keel over. Something to eat of any kind would go well, but a fat pig, within seventy-five yards, ready to be cleaned and cooked! John Lam- bert couldn't stand it, but, jumping out of the trenches, running back with the minnie balls cutting the dirt all around him, he succeeded in getting to that hog, grabbing it by the hind leg, and started back in face of death itself. No one expected him to get in, but on he came, and finally jumped in the trench, hog and all, without even a scratch. It was one of the most marvellous feats, besides the most daring, of anything that I recollect happening. After this if anything was ever said to John in reference to his being a *little scary* he would bring up the pig incident.

We remained in the trenches for some time before being relieved for a night, but at last our night came, and we were taken back to rest. We knew that Gen. Johnson Hagood's Brigade was somewhere on the line, and late in the afternoon Jim Diamond, Eddie Bellinger and myself got permission to go over to Hagood's brigade headquarters to see Vince Bellinger and Willie Hagood, who were in the brigade quartermaster department of Hagood's Brigade. We knew we would get something to eat and get something to bring back. We found them about sundown, and Vince and Willie told their man, Joe, a good old darkey, to commence preparing supper, and to fix enough of it. We sat around talking for a while, when Vince proposed that while Joe was fixing up the supper we should go right down the street to where he knew a fellow had something to drink. These boys were located near the town—in fact, at the head of a street.

We pulled out, and in a few minutes Vince knocked on a door on the street. Almost instantly the door was opened, and in all five of us went. There was a long counter on one side of the house. The old man had no lights except a tallow candle. We stepped up near the front and Vince called for the liquor. The old man set out a decanter with only about four drinks—when the old fellow filled up for the fifth man to get his—it was a half gallon decanter—then the last one of us poured his out, leaving the decanter full, except the one drink. We took our drink, and Vince asked how much. The old fellow said, "Ten dollars each," making fifty dollars for the treat. Vince gave him a one hundred dollar bill. He picked up his candle, going back to the end of the counter to his safe for the change; but in doing this he had left the decanter setting on the counter. I told Vince to walk back and get the change; we would walk out. I picked up the full decanter, and as we walked out the door Vince overtook us, and we all went out together.

However, we saw the old fellow, as he came back, hold up his light to look after his liquor. On discovering it gone, he jumped across the counter, following us. We were all in a dead run by this time. The old fellow was afraid to holler for police, as he was running what we now call a "blind tiger," but he followed us to the end of the street. When Vince picked up an old gun, and raising it, advanced on him, the old man then broke back as fast as he had come, leaving us with the liquor. We took another drink all around, when Joe told us to draw up, supper was ready. Joe had given us a good supper—hominy, fried bacon, biscuits and coffee—the best part of which was there was enough of it. We drank no more, for Vince and Willie asked us to carry some to Jim Hagood and Capt. Wood. They also told Joe to get us up some rations, and he put us up about a half of a side of bacon, about half a bushel of meal and some salt.

We got back to our command some time about midnight, and it was not long before Jim Hagood had his boy, Crow, and Pat Wood his boy, Fred, making up a fire, and about two o'clock we had a supper. In the meantime all the whiskey had disappeared. We all slept late next morning, and about eleven o'clock we had breakfast. We went back into the trenches and remained there some time, when we were taken across the James River to meet a demonstration being made there.

CHAPTER 12

Fort Harrison

It seems that our division (Fields'), especially our brigade, was selected and had ever been the troops to run from place to place. This
I egotistically claim was because we were good on the march, always
getting there quickly, and then, after getting there, we could be always depended upon to meet the emergency. Hence, we were not in
the trenches so continuously as some others. We, from now on, were
mostly below Richmond, taking care of Richmond from that side, but
occasionally we would run over and take a day or two in the trenches,
where we would be again pulled out for across the James River. So,
after about a week in the trenches on this occasion, we were taken
over the river, as Grant seemed to be preparing to attack from that
direction. We remained quietly, doing nothing but keeping out our
pickets for several days. For these few days we took up regular camp
duty, except drilling. At roll call in the mornings Morrison and Stewart hardly ever answered.

This got to be such a regular thing on all occasions, even when we
were called to move, that our orderly sergeant, A. P. Manville, became
so completely disgusted (for you could see disgust depicted on his
face) that it was determined between Perry Manville, Capt. Wood and
Col. Hagood that Morrison and Stewart should be assigned to me as
my company, I to see after them exclusively, being exempt from all
other duty, only go when they had to go, and *to make them go*. This
might seem an easy assignment, but, take my word for it, it was the
hardest job any poor fellow ever had. I would be up in the mornings
before time, getting them up to be in time for roll call, and any other
duties assigned them I would be notified and had to get them out for
it.

But Perry Manville, who was a brave, good fellow, would put them both on duty at the same time, thereby saving me extra duty. He saw and appreciated the hard task I had. After lying around here for perhaps a week or more watching and waiting we were ordered to "fall in." Our company was at this time on the left of the regiment, and I and my two men were on the extreme left, which, when marching left in front, put me and mine at the head next to the colonel. In starting out this time, when Col. Hagood rode up to his position, he turned to me and said, "Sergt. Mixson, load your gun immediately and take those two men in this fight or leave them dead on the wayside." I loaded up, telling these two what to expect from me (they had heard my orders).

We started off. I kept them up pretty well, and when we formed our line of battle on the hill overlooking Deep Bottom I had them in ranks. We remained on this hill while our skirmish line were holding them back in the bottom, our skirmishers retreating slowly. Gen. Lee was dismounted near us, awaiting the time to order us to charge. When it looked like the time had about come old Stewart got back pretty close to Gen. Lee, and, falling on his knees, said, "Let's all join in prayer," and he started off. He had hardly started good before the command was given, "Get to your places." Morrison went in ranks, but old man Stewart got louder. I called to him to get in. He got *louder*. I could not move him by calling, so I went up to him and, catching him by the shoulders, I pulled him back and almost had to drag him to his position. Lee looked on seemingly amused.

Well, we made the charge, meeting the enemy in the bottom. Here we fought them for some time, but finally retired to our former position on the hills. I don't think I got either Morrison or Stewart in this, but they were on hand when we got back on the hill. The enemy did not advance on us in our position, but fell back. We then went back and took up our quarters where we left the day before. Grant had failed here.

We remained here, without anything happening, doing picket duty and putting more logs on our fortifications, for something like three weeks, when the Yankees took another notion to go into Richmond over this route. Our cavalry, down at the Darbytown Road, discovered them on the move. As soon as this was reported to us our long roll routed us, and by sunrise we were off to look into matters. We ran upon their picket line about ten o'clock, drove them back and found them stationed behind the works that we had built there in 1862. We immediately charged these works, and took them with very little trouble, they giving way after a short fight. We followed them no further than the works we captured from them.

By night we were back at our camps, not much worse off than when we went out. We again took up our regular routine of duties and had no more disturbance from this quarter. Everything remaining quiet over here, we were, about the last of September or first of October, taken back to Petersburg and again went into the trenches. We were placed where the "blow up" afterwards took place, and while we were here our engineers were counter-sinking shafts, endeavouring to discover where the enemy's mine struck our fortifications.

The marksmen on the Yankee side had become very expert with both the rifle and mortars, and they were so accurate that mortar shells would frequently fall in our trenches. For the information of those who do not know about mortar shooting I will explain. The mortar gun is a short cannon, say eighteen inches long, working in a carriage on a pivot and so arranged as to be shot at any angle, even to straight up. They had perfected themselves so that they knew the exact elevation to give the gun and the length of the fuse to explode it, as in many instances the cannon ball would fall in our trenches, and, exploding, would do much harm, and causing much confusion among us.

Hence, it became necessary to keep a lookout, and when one of their guns was fired this "lookout" would keep his eye on the ball going up and coming over, and if it looked as if it were coming into the trenches at a certain place we would crowd away from the place that it seemed like hitting, thereby making room for it to fall and burst with as little damage as we had time and room to make.

On one occasion I was sitting with my back to the front of the trenches, flat down on the bottom of the trenches, with my oilcloth underneath me. I had my man Morrison as "lookout," who was kneeling down facing the front just at my side. I heard the report of a mortar and saw Morrison prick up his ears. Soon I saw him begin to get excited, and then he commenced to exclaim, "It's coming, it's coming, it's coming!" Knowing how scary he naturally was, I gave but little faith to him. His eyes, however, looked the size of saucers, and finally he fell over, exclaiming, "It's come," and the shell fell between my legs, my oilcloth keeping it from burying itself deep enough to retain it.

There I was, a shell with a burning fuse, in between my legs. It was death to do nothing, death to run, not only for me, but for others. It was impossible to get away from the shell, and instinct told me to get the shell away from me and us. Without having time to think even, I arose with the shell in my hands and dumped it out of the trenches. I scarcely had time to squat down when it bursted. Being outside, no one was hurt. I will take occasion to say here that this was no act of bravery. It was an inspiration that caused me to do it, and I was the worst scared fellow you ever saw, even more scared than Morrison or Stewart at any time. It took me a day or two to recover from the fright I got.

We remained in the trenches this time till about the first of November, when Grant again began to move around on the north side of the James. Then we were taken out and carried over, and it was well for us that it was so, for the day after we left the mine was sprung and many, very many, killed, and on the same ground we had been and just left. History will tell you of this. I was not there. On the day before the mine was sprung the Yankees on the north side of the James had charged and taken Fort Harrison, which was being held by the militia from Virginia. And on the morning that the mine was sprung they made an assault on Fort Gilmore, which was three miles from Fort Harrison, and garrisoned by veterans from Virginia.

The assault was made to draw our forces from the trenches, hoping to get enough away to make the springing of the mine a success, and to draw our attention elsewhere. We left the trenches late in the afternoon, and, passing Fort Harrison, leaving it to the right, went on to Fort Gilmore. We marched all night, arriving near Fort Gilmore at daybreak, when we halted and were held as a reserve. The assault was made by negro troops, with white officers with pistols in their hands, forcing the negroes forward on pain of death. They made a creditable charge, a good many jumping in the ditch in front of the fort. One charge, however, satisfied them.

About ten o'clock we went in and relieved the Virginians and remained there till after midnight, when we in turn were relieved and went down in front of Fort Harrison, arriving there just as day was breaking. On moving from Fort Gilmore to Fort Harrison, about three o'clock, before day, I took the company's canteens and went to a well we were passing and filled up. This got me some little behind, and going down the road to overtake our command a solitary horseman overtook me. I discovered at once it was Gen. Lee. He said, "What are you doing behind, my little fellow?" And when I told him I had stopped at the well just passed to fill the company's canteens he said, "Well, hurry and catch up; they will need you by daylight." When I did get up I told the boys we would have h——— by daylight, and told them that Gen. Lee had told me so.

In front of Fort Harrison we took our position in an old ditch trench which had been thrown up there perhaps a couple of years. This was not more than eight hundred yards in front of the fort. The Yankees had been reinforcing all night, and when day broke they were well garrisoned, with negro troops mostly. We remained in this position, awaiting the signal gun, when the advance on the Fort would be made from two sides. Tige Anderson's Georgians were to lead the charge on the front, supported by our brigade (Bratton's). Two other brigades were to attack the side. Capt. Wood's boy, Fred, brought in breakfast, and Capt. Wood, Eddie Bellinger and myself sat down to eat. Capt. Wood hurried through, leaving Eddie and me.

Then it was that Eddie said to me, "Frank, I will be killed this day. In an hour I will be a dead man." I told him if I felt that way I would go to Dr. Martin Bellinger, brigade surgeon, and be excused. He would not go. Just then the signal gun fired, and Tige Anderson, with his Georgians, led off, slowly at first. We were called to attention, and I missed Stewart. The negro boy, Fred, hearing me asking about him, said he had passed Mr. Stewart a mile back. I turned to Morrison and told him if he did not go this time I swear I would kill him. I intended to keep my eye on him. We were now ordered to advance. Anderson had started his charge, and as soon as we got straightened out, and after crossing the old ditch, we, too, charged.

Now the Yankees were mowing Anderson down with grape and canister, and we, being only a short distance behind, were getting the full benefit of every fire. I tell you, it was a grand sight to see our boy colonel. He was about the middle of the regiment, in front of it. We were at double quick. Jim Hagood kept his eyes on the fort, and when he saw smoke from a cannon, he would cry, "Down, First," at the same time falling flat himself. When the grape and canister had passed over he was the first up, and in that commanding voice, "Up, and forward, First." This he repeated more than half a dozen times. Anderson had now gotten to within about forty yards of the fort, where the firing was so fierce, furious and fatal. His men lay down. We kept on, and just before we reached them they commenced to holler to us to stop. Anderson was walking up and down, begging them to forward. Then he would curse them.

About now Lieut. Best, of our company, said, "Frank, I am shot through the thigh." I told him to go back. He said no. Only a step or two and he was shot clear through on the right side, the ball entering about the nipple. He now turned to go back, but just as he turned another ball hit him in the back, about an inch below where the other ball had come out, passing clear through, coming out where the other ball had entered. He now fell, and Sid Key, with another man with a litter, picked him up to take him off.

As they raised him up another ball knocked off two of his toes, making four wounds for him. I think he is still alive—was a few years ago, (as at time of first publication). When Lieut. Best fell we were passing through Anderson's brigade. I heard Anderson, as a last incentive to his men, say, "Georgia, you don't intend to let South Carolina beat you." I jumped up and hollered out, "Hurrah for South Carolina." But just as I struck the ground a ball struck me, and an old Georgian, who was lying flat on his belly, looking over his shoulder back at us, saw it and heard me, and said, "Oh, yes, G—— d——South Carolina, now."

This made such an impression on me that I have always believed that I would recognize that fellow's face wherever I saw it again. I was fortunately hit in the hand, breaking the knuckle of my forefinger on the left hand. I dropped my gun, and, running back to a pine, I got in behind it to examine how badly I was hurt, and when I discovered the bone shattered I pulled off my accoutrements, throwing them down, so I could have a good chance for running. Going only a short distance I heard the voice of Lieut. Col. Ben Kirkland, and I pulled up to see what was the matter. He was standing over an officer of our regiment, a captain, cursing him for all kinds of coward, and told him if he did not get up and go on with his company he would wear him out with his sword. I saw him get up, then I lit out again.

On getting back to where we had started, sitting there alone was Morrison, who told me that when Lieut. Best was hit he left. I went on a little back to where the field hospital was located (the field hospital is only to receive the wounded, staunch the blood of those who are likely to bleed to death, put them in an ambulance, sending them back to the general hospital). While hanging around there I noticed someone brought up on a litter, who, upon being put down, beckoned to me. I went up to him, failing at first to recognize him; but upon close inspection I discovered Capt. Wood. He was shot directly below his nose, the ball passing back lodged in the back of his neck, knocking out his teeth and lodging them in his tongue.

He was terribly disfigured at that time, but was operated on that night, they cutting out the ball from his neck, taking his teeth out of his tongue, etc. After the war he looked nearly as handsome as ever, and he was a handsome man.

I went on down from the field hospital to the regiment, after they were driven back, and it was a poor sight, indeed—only ninety-three men were left in the entire regiment. Eddie Bellinger had fallen, leading the regiment in about thirty yards of the fort. When the colonel ordered the regiment to fall back he discovered his colours missing and saw them on the ground nearer the fort than he was. He ran up there and found Eddie dead with the colours gripped so hard that he had to pry his fingers open with his sword to get them away. This all happened in thirty yards of the fort, in an open field.

The Yankees were so amazed at Col. Hagood's action that they did not shoot on him while he was doing this gallant deed. Col. Hagood then called Jim Diamond, who was not wounded, and turned the colours over to him. He brought them out. Next day the Yankees sent over a flag of truce, asking the name of the gallant officer who had rescued the colours—they buried Eddie with military honours.

I did not get my wound dressed until the day after the fight. That evening I went back to the general hospital. Dr. Wallace Bailey, from the Four Mile, our surgeon, glanced at it casually and told me he would cut off the finger when he had time—the surgeons were all busy that evening, all night and next day. Capt. Wood was operated on during the night and looked badly next morning. Many a poor fellow lost an arm or a leg out here. That night this hospital was cleaned up, all of us being loaded on boats and sent to the hospital in Richmond, reaching there some time about midnight, and were immediately unloaded into a large kind of warehouse that had been prepared with cots, etc., for a kind of reception hospital. Here we were seen after by the ladies, our wounds dressed, and nourishment given us. Those who were not too badly wounded were sent on next day to the regular hospital. I did not let Dr. Bailey cut off my finger. *I have it yet.*

CHAPTER 13

Wounded & An Execution

In the hospital at Richmond I was assigned to a ward that a Dr. Wilson, of Marion, S. C., was in charge of. This doctor seemed to take a liking to me from the start—I guess on account of my age and size. Some three or four days after my arrival there he told me the Examining Board would meet next day. This board would look over the wounded and furlough those who would be disqualified long enough to go home, and he said he would put me on the list to go before this board. My hopes were high and I could scarcely await the time with patience. But ten o'clock finally came, and the crowd began to gather. The board met in a large one-room building, one door on the side, another on the end. The board consisted of five members, the chairman of which was an old man. Their position in the room was in chairs towards the end, opposite the end door. They had a clerk, who had listed all names of those were applying. This clerk had a doorkeeper, and he would take off the list as he had them entered, call the name to his doorkeeper, who would extend the call and admit the man.

After a long wait, my name was called and I went in fully confident that I would get a furlough. I was called over to where the doctors were sitting in a row, and the old doctor told me to show up. I readily did so, and when they saw that I was wounded in the hand, he, the old doctor, said, "Pass out." I can tell you, I was disappointed, and so was Dr. Wilson; but he consoled me with the information that the Board would meet again in a few days and to try them again. This I did with the same result, only this time they did not even condescend to look at my hand. In a few days they again met, and again I went before them. But this time they didn't even allow me to stop, but as I walked in one door the old doctor waved me out of the other.

This I reported to Dr. Wilson. He told me they treated me this way because so many were shooting themselves in the hands and feet to get out of service even for a time. After getting this information I went over to the officers' hospital and got a certificate signed by Capt. Wood and Lieut. Best, and got Dr. Bellinger, who came over to see how all his men were doing, to give me one, and then Col. Hagood sent his certificate to me. In the meantime, Dr. Wilson had told me to let my hand and arm lay so that the warm sun could shine through the glass on it. After doing this a couple of days my arm began to swell and turn red and the middle of my hand had become somewhat inflamed. So now I was fixed for the next meeting.

The day soon came, and early in the morning Dr. Wilson called me to him and stuck a lancet in the middle of my hand, put cotton on it and wrapped it up, telling me not get out of the board room without showing all I had. When I was called this time, as I walked in the door, the old doctor again waved me to the other door; but instead of obeying him I went over to them and asked that they look at my hand. They agreed, when I undid it and pulled off the cotton. It began to bleed. Then I pulled up my sleeve, showing them my red, swollen arm. After seeing this they consulted and told me they were sorry that it was so they could not furlough me. I certainly deserved it. I then went down in my breeches pocket and brought out those certificates, which I handed them.

After reading these the old doctor said to his clerk, "Give him thirty days." I do believe Dr. Wilson was as much pleased as I was, and he got my papers for me and got me off that same night, making me twenty-four hours ahead. I left Richmond that night on a crowded train. I got a seat with a poor fellow who had just had his leg cut off, and I helped him on his way, getting him water, dividing my rations with him and at nearly all the stations home the women would be at the depots with something to eat for us wounded. I kept the old fellow in good shape up to Williston, where I left him.

I was so accustomed to walking that I did not even ask anyone at Williston to send me home. It was only fourteen miles anyway, and I had no baggage of any kind, so I did not feel that I had much before me. I reached home in due time, and mother and my sisters all seemed mighty glad to see me. They had heard of the Fort Harrison fight and slaughter, and heard that we were in it; and had even heard of some of the killed and wounded, but had heard nothing from me and had decided that "no news is good news." Hence, they were not surprised to see me.

After remaining home with my own people a few days I went up on the Four Mile to see Mr. and Mrs. Wilson, *my other people*. I remained there for about ten days when I went back home. It was not much longer now before my thirty days' would expire and I determined to be back to my command on time. When my sisters knew that I had been appointed a sergeant nothing would do but that they should put the stripes on my sleeves. I didn't care to have it done, but they put them on anyway.

Well, the time came for me to go back, and when I got to Williston to take the train it seemed as if I had a wagon load of boxes filled with everything good to eat and clothes to wear. There was a box for Sid Key, Ed. Harley, Job Rountree, Jno. Williams Canady, Darling Sprawls, Bill Kitchins, Mathias Hair, old man Walton Hair, Frank and Jno. Green, W. W. Woodward, Darius Ogden, and perhaps others whom I can't recall. Of course, I had one for myself. How I ever managed to get these to the camps I don't know, but they all did get there, and, it being not long till Christmas, old Company E had a regular "jollification." There were a few members of the company who did not live near me and did not get any box by me; but, all the same, those who had divided with them, and the entire company fared well for a while.

I found our command still below Richmond. I walked over from Richmond and struck the line up on the hill, and discovered that our brigade was down towards the left. I passed on down the line. Now, there were nice breastworks on the front, built out of logs. The quarters for the men were some of logs, some with logs covered with tents and some with tents only, situated in some one hundred yards in rear of the works. The space between the works and the quarters was used for a drill ground and a general street. Down this street I had to go. I had not gone far before some fellow cried out, "Here goes the dominecker sergeant," and in no time you could hear it for a mile ahead, "Here comes the dominecker sergeant." Then it was that I cursed myself for having on those stripes. I was not fit for duty for several weeks after getting back, but did take charge of *my company*, however—Morrison and Stewart.

Things about now were looking squally for our cause and a good many of our army were getting worn out and discouraged. The reports from Johnston's army made matters look more gloomy, and as time went on Sherman commenced his raid, going to Savannah and then turning up and entering South Carolina. Our men with families at home, who were being left homeless and in a starving condition, were very much disheartened and discouraged. Some desertions were made. I remember among the first was a man named Mack, from Orangeburg. He had heard very distressing news from his wife and children, and, failing to get a furlough, he determined to go to them. He was brought back, tried by court-martial, convicted and sentenced to be shot. I can never forget that day.

The entire corps was turned out in a large open field and formed in a hollow square. Twelve men from our regiment were drawn on the shooting detail. I was the sergeant on the detail. My duty was to have these twelve men march out twenty paces from the stake erected where the man Mack was to be placed. When reaching this position I had the twelve men stack their arms, then I moved them back out of sight and turned them over to Lieut. Southern, who was in charge of them for the execution. I then went back to the stacked arms and loaded the guns, putting blank cartridges in six and loaded cartridges in six, and restacking them.

Then in this square a wagon drove in. On this wagon was Mack, sitting on his coffin. On each side of the wagon was a guard; in rear of the wagon was the band. This procession started off at one end of the hollow square; moving to the right, the band playing the death march. They went all round the entire square, giving each and every man a good opportunity of viewing it. At last they arrived at the other end of the square, when Mack, without assistance, got off the wagon and walked to the stake. The coffin was placed just in rear; then Mack was asked to kneel down with his back to the stake, and he was tied to it with a plough line. He was blindfolded. Now Lieut. Southern, with his twelve men, was seen to enter the square at a quick step and was halted at the stacked arms.

Lieut. Southern gave the command, as follows: "Attention, detail. Take arms. Carry arms. Ready—aim—fire!" At the report of the twelve guns poor Mack's head fell on his chest—he was a dead man. Lieut. Southern immediately moved his men off, so that they would see as little of it as possible, taking them back, disbanded them to their different commands. This ended the first and last lesson we ever got for desertion. It was hard to see, but such had to be, else our officers, from poor Mack's captain, his colonel, brigadier general, up to the Christian soldier, Bob Lee, would never have allowed it.

Appomattox

Some little time after this I was the sergeant on the picket line. The enemy's line of picket was some four hundred yards off, but in fair view. At midnight I sent William Dyches, a private from Company E, to relieve the vidette and to remain as vidette till day began to break, then to come back to our picket line. Just as day had fairly broken and Dyches had not come in I took a look for him, and was surprised to see him nearly over to the Yankees. I took a shot at him, but missed him. A Yankee then hollered over to me, saying, "Say, Johnny, we've got one of your small potatoes." I replied, "D——d small, but few in a hill." Dyches had always been a very good soldier—had never shirked duty and was ever there in a fight. He was from the section of Barnwell district, now Aiken County, known as Cracker's Neck, near the Upper Three Runs. Dyches did not reach home until after we all had surrendered and tramped from Appomattox home.

We never went back to the trenches after the charge on Fort Harrison; remaining, however, below Richmond until the night of April 1st, when we abandoned our quarters, gave up our breastworks and took our march for Richmond. We reached Richmond after midnight and everything was in confusion and uproar—the city was on fire in more than one place. Soldiers on horse and on foot were going in every direction—old men and women and children were on the streets weeping; all that, together with the heavy firing we could hear at Petersburg, told us that Richmond was gone—Richmond, the goal that Grant had striven so hard for and for which he had sacrificed so many lives, would be his at last. In passing through Richmond I lost both Morrison and Stewart—they escaped me in the confusion.

We went on through Richmond, giving it up to the Yankees who entered just behind us, and just before noon we reached Petersburg.

Here we found our troops hardly pressed. We were placed in position some four or five hundred yards below the bridge which spanned the Appomattox River, with orders to hold the bridge, as it was the only escape our whole army had, and to lose this we were captured. We held the advancing enemy all the afternoon until late into the night after our army had crossed. We were drawn off and crossed over, then, pouring oil on the bridge, set fire to it. After seeing it in flames we took up our march as rear guard to Lee's army on that ever-to-be-remembered six days' march, *and every hour a fight* to Appomattox.

I don't know how to tell of this march. Things happened so fast and we were pressed so hard that we were at one place for only a few minutes and then at another. In a fight here, holding the enemy back long enough for our troops to cross a stream, or even a narrow place in the road, then we were gone. I know at Farmville we had a good, stiff fight, holding the enemy back while our troops crossed the bridge, and at one time it seemed that they would cut us off. Some of our troops waded the creek, neck deep.

After passing this place just on top of the hill we found our quartermaster and commissary wagons deserted and afire. Just a little further on we stopped to blow, and I made up a fire and beat up some batter, put a flap-jack in the frying pan. Just as it was ready to turn over we were ordered to make a quick charge. I grabbed my frying pan, flap-jack and all, and went into the charge. We drove the Yankees back, and, getting back to my fire, I finished cooking my flap-jack, and it ate right well.

For six days and six nights we did not stop for sleep nor for rest longer than ten minutes, but those ten minutes were used for sleep. It was a fight and a run the whole time. I saw men—and I did the thing myself—go to sleep walking along. Two days before reaching Appomattox Frank Green slipped out on the side, to see if he could get something to eat. He got off some half mile and had succeeded in getting a half middling of bacon from an old woman. He stuck his bayonet through this and swung it on his shoulder and started out for us. He soon discovered that the Yankees' cavalry were between him and us. He therefore had to outmanoeuvre them some way. Being in any open country this was hard to do. Two of them soon spied him and went for him; but, after an hour or more, Frank came in *with his bacon, too.*

Along about now I was again barefoot. I had not had an opportunity to run upon any dead Yankees, as *we were doing the running these times*. So I commenced looking around for a pair of shoes somewhere. I soon discovered that Sid Key had a pair of number sixes hung onto his belt. Sid wore about tens. I bartered him for a trade. He was willing to sell, but he wanted cash. However, he let me have them on credit, with the understanding that I would pay him after the next fight if I got anything from a dead Yankee. We never got into another fight *where we held the field*, consequently, I never had a chance at a dead Yankee; and I owe Sid for those shoes yet!

On the morning of April 9th, 1865, we were halted in a field. Firing was going on down on the front. We had not long stopped when we noticed that the firing on the front had ceased. We were lying down on each side of the road. Presently we saw two men galloping up the road. On reaching us we discovered one to be one of our general's staff officers, the other to be a Yankee officer. Right then there was excitement. We knew something was wrong, but what was it? Sleep and exhaustion had gone; everybody was up, stirring around and wondering. We were held here in this position and under this strain for over three hours, when the report got started that *Lee had surrendered*. Very shortly after we heard this we saw a crowd of horsemen coming up the road.

We soon recognized Gen. Lee among them. Every man got on his feet, and we commenced yelling for Lee. The old man pulled off his hat, and, with tears streaming down his cheeks, without a word, he rode through us. Lee was not the only one shedding tears—old men who had wives, sons, daughters, even grandchildren at home; middle aged men who had families at home; younger men who had left a young wife, and young fellows like myself—all were bowing their heads with tears; but no thought of censure; no criticism of Gen. Lee, ever entered the minds of any of us. We knew he had done for the best and we had more confidence in him, as he rode through us that day, than we ever had before, and we loved him more. We knew how humiliated he felt, and, knowing this, we were anxious to make him feel that we recognized that he had done right, and our confidence and love for him, instead of being shaken, had been increased. He was certainly now more of an idol than ever before.

That afternoon we were taken into the oak grove and put in the Bull Pen, as we called it. This was only going into bivouac with a guard around us, *but not a Yankee guard*. We could not have submitted to that had that been attempted; the last one would have been knocked out during the night. But we had our own men for our guards. We were not allowed out of our lines, nor were any Yankees allowed to come in; but they hung around and seemed surprised that they had such a hard time in overwhelming such a crowd of rag-a-muffins, and so few of them.

On being put into the Bull Pen it so happened, and we immediately discovered, there was in our regimental lines a large barn pretty well filled with ears of corn. We were soon scrambling for this and men could be seen going in all directions with an armful of this corn. It looked exactly like each man was going to feed a horse. It was well for us that we struck this luck, for we had nothing to eat; and when there is nothing better, parched corn goes mighty good. We now filled up on our parched corn and by good dark everybody seemed to be asleep—the first sleep we had for seven days and nights, since we left Richmond. We awoke the next morning, and, after taking our breakfast (parched corn again and water), we felt very much refreshed, after a night of sleep and rest. We would hang around our lines, seeing anything that might take place.

During the morning Gen. Lee, accompanied by Gen. Meade and staff, rode around. I suppose Gen. Lee was showing Gen. Meade how few men he had surrendered him and the condition they were in. On passing by us we began to cheer and yell. Meade turned to his colour bearer, who had his headquarters' flag rolled up, and said, "Unfurl that flag." This he did, when an old, ragged, half-starved, worn-out Confederate soldier in our lines cried out, "D——n you old rag. We are cheering Gen. Lee." This old fellow, like the balance of us, was no more whipped, penned up here in the Bull Pen, overpowered by at least ten to one, starved, naked, broken down, than he was at the Wilderness, Spotsylvania, Cold Harbor or the nine months in the trenches and below Richmond.

We were not whipped, and we never felt whipped; but felt like men who had done their duty in every emergency, and now, while we were forced to give up the struggle, it was only to overwhelming odds and resources. But we were yet men and men, too, who were entitled to and would get the admiration of the entire world. We knew we deserved this, and, knowing it, we held up our heads, not ashamed to look our victors straight in the eye. *And they, the Yankees*, acted with much consideration, and like good soldiers, and good Americans can only act, did not show that exultation they must have felt. While they seemed to feel proud, of course, at the result, yet we had their sympathy and good will.

This was April 10. We remained in our lines the entire day. To this we did not object, as we needed the rest, and, besides, we did not care to move around much. Again, we had a good night's sleep and parched corn enough to eat. Early on the morning of the 11th it became known that we were to be taken out and surrender our arms, ammunition and everything else. We were, however, allowed to retain our side arms and blankets. The side arms consisted of, with the officer, his sword and pistol; with the private, his haversack, canteen and little hand axe, the axe that we wore stuck in our belts and which had been of so much service to us in building log breastworks at the Wilderness, Spotsylvania, Cold Harbor, Petersburg and below Richmond.

We noticed in the morning, say ten o'clock, the Yankee columns moving down to Appomattox Court House. At noon our drums beat for us to fall in. In a short time we were again in ranks. Lee's army was now moving down the road towards Appomattox Court House, every man fully armed, cartridge boxes full and the men well rested. We knew we were being taken to stack and give up those arms which had been a part of us for four long years; but we did not lag or skulk. Had Gen. Lee, then and there, ridden out and said, "Boys, there are the enemy, go for them," there would have been no man to question it; we would have broken through, no matter the odds.

But we marched up in front of them, where they were formed in line of battle, with our heads up, showing them that a soldier knows how to die. We were stopped and made to face them, and then, for the last time, we heard our boy colonel, Jim Hagood, give the command, "First South Carolina, order arms, fix bayonets, stack arms, unbuckle accoutrements, hang up accoutrements."

When this was completed we heard again his command, "First Regiment, attention. Right face, file right, march."

The deed was done. Now we were truly prisoners—nothing with which to protect us from either danger or insult. We were carried back from whence we came, and we took up our quarters as before. We suffered no insult in any way from any of our enemies. *No other army in the world would have been so considerate* of a foe that it had taken so long, so much privation, so much sacrifice of human life, to overwhelm. Gen. Grant had acted nobly towards Gen. Lee. His men acted considerately towards us.

That evening Col. Hagood got enough paroles for the men of his regiment, but did not give them out. The next day, April 12, Col. Hagood, having decided to try the scheme of keeping us together, started

OUR BOY COLONEL.

James R. Hagood

Colonel of (Hagood's) First S. C. Regiment of Volunteer Infantry, C. S. Army.

Of him General Lee wrote as follows:—

> It gives me pleasure to state that Col. J. R. Hagood, during the whole term of his connection with the Army of Northern Virginia, was conspicuous for gallantry, efficiency and good conduct. By his merit constantly exhibited, he rose from a private in his regiment to its command, and showed by his actions that he was worthy of the position.
>
> (Signed) R. E. Lee.
>
> Lexington, Va., 25th March, 1868.

J. R. Hagood volunteered as a private in the above named regiment, just before its departure to Virginia, in the summer of 1862, under the command of Col. Thomas Glover, who had succeeded Johnson Hagood to the colonelcy of the regiment upon the latter's promotion to brigadier-general.

J. R. Hagood was promoted sergeant-major of the regiment August, 1862. He was promoted adjutant of the regiment November 16th, 1862. He was promoted captain of Company K January, 1863. He was promoted colonel of the regiment on 16th of November, 1863. His commission being dated within ten days of his nineteenth birthday, he was doubtless the youngest colonel commanding a regiment in the Confederate Army.

This rapid promotion came to him while serving in and forming a part of "that incomparable infantry which bore upon its bayonets the failing fortune of the Confederacy for four long and bloody years." He surrendered at Appomattox, with Lee's army, having participated in nineteen battles in which at least 20,000 men were engaged.

the tramp for home. Early in the morning the Yankees had sent us over some beef, and upon dividing this out each man got one-fourth of a pound. This was the only rations we had issued to us during the time we were in the Bull Pen; but, in justice to the enemy, I must say that they, too, had not had anything issued them.

I guess we had travelled so fast and furiously that their wagon could not keep up. Here we were, six hundred miles away from home, not a cent in our pockets, and only one-fourth of a pound of raw beef. Can a more deplorable picture be drawn? Col. Hagood marched us off, keeping us pretty well together till night coming on we stopped. We had travelled about twenty miles towards home this day. After stopping for the night Col. Hagood called on the few officers present to meet him, when he explained that we had no money nor had we authority to confiscate something to eat. The men now had nothing and hadn't had for over ten days.

He had thought it best to keep them together as long as possible, and now he had gotten them some twenty miles away from the Yankee army, he saw no other alternative but to give each man his parole and turn him loose to get home the best he could. He was satisfied this was the best course. All the officers present agreed with him, and that night each orderly sergeant was given the number of paroles to be filled out, inserting the man's name. By midnight Orderly Sergeant A. P. Manville and myself had them all ready for Company E, and early next morning Sergt. Manville called up the company and gave to each man his parole. Then, with tears in our eyes, we bade each other goodbye, and took our course for our desolated homes in old Barnwell District.

CHAPTER 15

The Tramp Home

Jim Diamond and I did as we had always done—joined our fortunes—and taking a kind of byway we soon were away from any soldiers. We considered it so much better to leave the highways and public roads, as on the private ways we would stand a much better chance to get something to eat. We found this plan to work very well, and during the whole distance and time we took to get home we never went hungry. At times we would strike a highway for a short distance when we would run upon a lot of fellows tramping for their homes, some of whom had to go so far as Texas. How they ever lasted that long and held out to make such a distance I can't conceive.

We would generally stop at nearly every house we passed and beg for something to eat, or for milk or buttermilk; and there being only two of us, we were hardly ever refused, consequently, we never wanted. After so long a time we were in the neighbourhood of Danville, Va. We concluded to go by and take in the place and see what was going on there. We reached Danville early in the morning and found an immense crowd—it seemed that all of us had taken in the place.

Not long after we reached the city we determined to charge a store in which there were some government goods, and a big crowd soon gathered. It did not take long to batter down the doors and get in. Then the scramble began. There were bacon, meal, molasses, clothes, blankets and everything else. The way the men got the molasses was by knocking out the head of the hogshead and dipping in their canteens. In one instance the pressure around a hogshead was so great that one fellow next to the barrel, being pressed so tight, was raised off his feet; but he deliberately stepped over into the barrel, standing up in the molasses to his waist. He filled his canteen and then crawled out.

Jim and I got in this raid a small piece of bacon, some meal, a couple of army blankets and a McClelland saddle. We then went on down town to the depot and found a train of cars standing on the track headed southwards. The engine was fired up and every available space, inside and outside and on top, was taken, and all that was necessary to move off was an engineer. Just away from where this train stood was a magazine, filled with all manner of explosive missiles. In some manner this magazine caught and soon the explosion occurred and pieces of shells were flying in every direction.

Then those who were on the train began to get away—some even jumping through the car windows, others from the top. While this was at its worst a Texan jumped on the engine and cried out, "I am an engineer; I can run it. Give me a fireman." Immediately someone answered his call. In the meantime, as the others jumped off, making room, Jim and I got on, and our Texas engineer pulled out amid the confusion from the live magazine. Whether he knew much about handling an engine or not, he did certainly let it run, stopping for no place nor for nothing, until just before reaching Salisbury, N. C., an axle to the tender broke. This, of course, put an end to our ride. Deserting the train, leaving it on the track, we again pulled out afoot. We had, however, made a good many miles, which did us much good. In due course of time we struck the neighbourhood of Charlotte, N. C., and desired to "take in" that city, too, for we wanted to see and hear what might be going on in the world, we having confined all our movements to country roads and country houses.

We went into Charlotte, and, having our haversacks well filled, we were in no hurry. We loafed around the town taking in the sights. Here again we met a large crowd of Lee's paroled men, and here again we made a raid on some government stores. But as we had plenty to eat we didn't take much hand in it. However, we got a bolt of real good jeans—about all we did get.

Jim had traded his saddle before reaching Charlotte, consequently, we were not hampered with carrying that. We left the city before dark and continued our course south, regardless of where we would strike next. Sometimes we had to go some distance to get a ferry across a river, and in one or two instances a farmer would take us over in his *batteau*. We were faring right well, and, as neither of us had a wife and children awaiting our coming, we did not push hard after leaving Charlotte. The next town I recollect passing through was Newberry. We heard of the assassination of President Lincoln at Charlotte. On reaching Newberry early in the morning we were the wonder of the town. They had not heard of the surrender of Lee nor of Lincoln's death. It seemed as if the town turned out to see us.

We stopped here only long enough for Jim to get a shave, the barber doing it for nothing. We slept in a farmer's barn that night about eight miles from Newberry. This farmer gave us supper and next morning breakfast. And we went on our way rejoicing. Our next stop was at a farmer's house in now Saluda County—Mr. Ready— on the Columbia and Augusta Railroad. He was an old bachelor and made us come in his house, giving us supper, bed and breakfast, and an early start the next morning. Besides, he gave us directions how to get to Pine Log Bridge, across the Edisto River.

We crossed the Edisto in the afternoon and took that big old sandy road for White Pond. Reaching that place, just before sundown, we went on our way, and between sundown and dark we stopped at a little log cabin, asking for something to eat and telling the lady, Mrs. Beach, that we would sleep in the pines. This she would not consent to, but made us walk in, prepared supper, made us down a pallet in front of the fire. Before going to bed she told us her husband was a soldier, too, belonging to Lamar's Second South Carolina Artillery, with Johnston's army. She had not heard from him since they left Charleston. Beach did get home all right.

Next morning she was up bright and early and gave us breakfast and Godspeed. It was now only a few miles before we would reach the forks of the road where Jim and I would part, he going to Barnwell and I to Joyce's Branch, ten miles above Barnwell. The nearer we reached this fork of the road the more serious we would become. We had eaten and slept together for nearly three years—had shared privations together, and in prosperity we divided with each other; and now, we were on the verge of parting, perhaps never to see each other again. We had been passing the burnt houses, done by Sherman in his march, and we did not know what we might find at our homes; but we well knew there were hard times ahead of us.

At last, we arrived at the parting place, and, by common instinct, we determined to make the parting short. Jim took the bolt of jeans from his shoulders, where he had it slung, told me to pull it out, and then, doubling it in the middle, cut it in two. *This was all.* Without saying a word more, we shook hands and turned off quickly. Jim had about twelve miles to Barnwell; I about ten to Joyce's Branch. I reached home just as they had finished dinner. They, too, had not heard of Lee's surrender. They hunted me up some old clothes, sent me to an outhouse to wash and clean up, and then buried my suit of Confederate gray, as that was the best thing to do with it. I was very much gratified to find that Sherman's raiders had not gotten as high up as our place. The nearest they came, however, was only one and a half miles off towards Barnwell. I found that none of our negroes had run off, but all were at home making a crop, and mother had a good supply of "hog and hominy."

There were, however, about a dozen cases of smallpox on the place, left by some straggler, the most of which was among the negroes. I was not afraid of it, having been well vaccinated while below Richmond, and I did not hesitate to go right in to it and help all those who had it, both white and black. It was but a few days before my sisters had me a real nice suit of clothes, made from the jeans we had raided at Charlotte and divided at the forks of the road. The first time I went to Barnwell I saw Jim Diamond in his suit made from the other part.

Now, the war is over, and we are again civilians. My reminiscences of a private are at an end. There are things I should have written in these had they occurred to me at the right time, and perhaps there are things that might have been left out. But when I would take my seat to write I did not know what I intended saying. It seemed to come to me by inspiration, and I would just write as fast as pencil could go. I will have to ask the public to be charitable in reading this. Recollect, I went into the war a mere country boy, fourteen and a half years old, and returned to a ruined, desolate and impoverished country at eighteen years and six months old.

Reminiscence of Four Years as a Private
Soldier

JOHN GILL

Contents

Notice

This little pamphlet is printed for my own pleasure and use, without pretence to historical accuracy—it is a personal reminiscence only.

A few copies will be printed for my immediate family and friends.

The matter contained has been jotted down at odd moments as the memory of days long ago came back to me.

John Gill.

Dedicated to the memory of my dear brother,
who gave his life to the cause of the South.
He sleeps on the battlefield,
but will awaken at the call of the redeemed,
and be blessed for evermore.

*There is a bright abode reserved
for all good soldiers who die in action.*

Memoirs

My grandfather, John Gill, of Alexandria, Virginia, the son of Thomas Gill of Notton, Yorkshire, England, came to this country just after the close of the American Revolution, as the resident partner of the shipping firm of Abernethy, Lowry & Gill, of London, one of the leading firms of that time.

My grandmother Gill was Esther Lowry, daughter of Col. William Lowry and Olivia Pickens, his wife, both from Castle Blaney, County Monaghan, Ireland.

Colonel Lowry came to Baltimore in 1794, and shortly after was commissioned by Governor Lee, of Maryland, Major of the 27th Regiment, Maryland Volunteers. He was subsequently made colonel of the regiment.

His son, J. Lowry Donaldson, was adjutant of the 27th Regiment in the Battle of North Point, in which he was killed. He was a distinguished lawyer and a member of the Mary- land Legislature. His name was changed by an Act of Assembly from Lowry to Donaldson, in compliance with the request of a rich uncle of that name, residing in London.

My father was Richard W. Gill, son of John Gill, of Alexandria, Virginia. My mother was Ann E. Deale, daughter of Captain James Deale, West River, Anne Arundel County, Md. My great grandfather. Captain John Deale, was an officer in the 31st Weems Battalion, and served during the Revolution in defence of Annapolis and that portion of the county bordering on the Chesapeake Bay. My maternal grandmother was a Franklin, whose family were large property and slave owners in Anne Arundel County.

I was born August 15, 1841, in the City of Annapolis. My father died February 28, 1852, when I was only ten years old.

My mother was left with four children, two girls and two boys.

Fortunately my father had left an estate sufficient to provide comfortably for all of us, and my mother, being a woman of most excellent sense and judgment, made the best possible disposition of her income with the view of educating her children.

My father's death left a scar that time could never efface. One of his associates at the bar, in announcing his death to a full bench of the Court of Appeals of Maryland, said: "I will not attempt to eulogize the dead, but I cannot refrain from saying that I have never known one who more deservedly and universally possessed the esteem of all who knew him."

For several years after my father's death we were all kept at home. My mother had secured a most excellent governess, a Miss Boyce, who proved most satisfactory and was liked so much that she soon became part of our household.

At the age of about 15 I was sent to the Preparatory School of St. John's College. In 1856 my mother and sisters concluded that it was best for me to go to a boarding-school, and the Lawrenceville High School, near Princeton, New Jersey, was selected.

I shall never cease being grateful to my dear mother for sending me to this school. At the head of it was a very distinguished educator, Dr. Samuel Hamill, well known throughout the country, and the best man I ever knew to train boys in the way they should go.

I graduated at Lawrenceville during the fall of 1859, and from there went to the University of Virginia.

At the outbreak of the Civil War, 1861, I enlisted as a private soldier in the Confederate Army.

All things have worked together for my good.

CHAPTER 1

Escape to Virginia

It was forty-two years ago last spring since the first mutterings of the Civil War alarmed the country. Already several of the Southern States had withdrawn from the Union, and in the early part of 1861 it was evident that others would soon follow.

As I was born a Marylander, my early education and training pointed in one direction. My family for many years, especially on my mother's side, had owned slaves, and I had never been taught to believe that slavery was a sin or a crime. All my early sympathies and associations were decidedly averse from these opinions.

Therefore, when the question as to the right of these States to separate peaceably from the compact formed by their forefathers was resisted and denied by one section of the country, I was not long in deciding the question for myself. I determined at once which cause to espouse, and to take up arms to defend it. I was a mere boy at the time, scarcely nineteen years of age. Two years before my mother had sent me to the University of Virginia, hoping that my education would someday fit me, in some small degree, to follow in the footsteps of my illustrious father, who, although dead ten years before the outbreak of the war, had left behind him an enviable reputation for high character and distinguished services to his State as a jurist and useful citizen.

While at the University I formed many early attachments, especially among the Southern students, and when the issue arose I felt their destiny to be my destiny. Oh, how bright and happy were the days preceding the war! what pleasant associations still ring out from those old University walls! How little did we know, or how little did we think what a change would soon take place; what the magnitude of that change would be! Some predicted a short war; the issue would soon be settled in a few months. Others shook their heads and looked aghast at the prospect before them. Well, the war lasted four years, four long, dreary years, years of trials and hardships unequalled in the annals of war.

We were told when we were schoolboys that our forefathers in the struggle for American independence, suffered and endured every privation, but when I compare the events of these two epochs, I question very much if their trials were greater than ours; at least I hope not.

The country was now thoroughly aroused. Fort Sumter had been fired upon, and both sides were calling for volunteers. Mr. Lincoln had issued his proclamation for 75,000 troops. The South was not idle. The call to arms was heard throughout the land.

On the part of the North, troops were being rapidly moved forward to Washington to defend the National Capital. The Southerners were concentrating in the vicinity of Richmond, Virginia, to defend that city, which was to become the capital of the new Confederacy.

I had returned to Baltimore, and found great excitement throughout the State. In an effort to pass Northern soldiers through the city, men of Southern sympathy arose and organized to resist. On the 19th of April, 1861, the 6th Massachusetts Regiment, which was marching up Pratt street from the President Street Station to the B. & O. depot, were fired upon and severely handled by an excited mob. Maryland was now thoroughly aroused and realized that all State rights were ignored by the general government, and if not already she would soon be under bayonet rule.

There was a general call to arms, and troops were sent to the Susquehanna to destroy the bridge over that river. Every obstacle was devised to retard Northern troops reaching Washington. I became a member of the Maryland guard. We were drilled day and night to get ready to fight and resist any further attempt to pass soldiers through the State. While this was going on, a large body of troops was being transported from Havre de Grace by water to Annapolis, and thence by rail to Washington. In this way, in a short time, Maryland had a large hostile army to hold her in subjection, and those of her sons who were still ready to fight for her soon realized that they could fight only by removing the seat of war south of the Potomac River.

I concluded at once to start south. The first thing to do was to go to Annapolis, the place of my birth, my old home, and say goodbye to my mother and sister, who were supposed to be still there. I had had no communication with them for a week or ten days, and took it for granted that they were at home. Imagine my deep regret, therefore, upon arriving at Annapolis, to find that they had left the city on one of the government transports bound for New London. Many citizens of Annapolis, especially those connected with the army and navy, had availed themselves of this opportunity to remove their families to a place of safety and far away from the seat of war.

My mother and sister had many friends among the officers of the navy, and it was through the kindness of Captain Joseph Miller that they were cared for in this good manner.

What a crushing blow to me not to see my dear mother! But it has often occurred to me since that it was just as well that we did not meet, as the parting would have been heartbreaking in the extreme. This was about May the 1st, when most of my friends and relatives had fled from the city. I ventured, however, before getting my horse, which had been engaged at a livery stable, to go down to the academy, to say farewell to some of my old friends and inform them of my intentions, some of whom I should never see again.

I shall never forget that night. Notwithstanding the fact that I was soon to take up arms against the government, these old friends were friends still, and it was trying to break the cord which had so long united us in friendly and social intercourse.

Midnight was rapidly approaching when I went to the stable, and mounting my horse rode away to South River. On coming to the ferry, the ferryman of course was asleep and no boat was crossing at that hour. However, I soon roused him up, and he knew, without asking me, what I was after and what I was doing. I paid him the ferriage, and said goodbye. I think he would have been delighted to go with me, but we exchanged very few remarks about the war.

I rode on to Cedar Park, the ancestral home of the Mercers. Arriving there early in the morning, some hours before breakfast, I had time to put up my horse and prepare myself a little before being presented to the ladies.

In regard to West river, there are very few people in Maryland today who can recall what West River was before the war. It was a thickly settled agricultural and aristocratic, neighbourhood, situated between Rhodes and West Rivers, forming a peninsula, and the land was owned by some of the most cultivated and attractive people in the State, containing some of the oldest families: the Mercers, Markoes, Hughes, Maxcys, Deales, Contees, Steuarts, Chestons, Murrays, Brogdens, Sellmans, Steeles and Franklins. Some of the estates were extremely well kept, and were the frequent scenes of great social gatherings at certain seasons of the year. Cedar Park was particularly noted for its hospitality and charming daughters.

As before stated, I had arrived early in the morning and was already standing in the hall when first to welcome me appeared the charming hostess of the house, Mrs. Mercer. She was soon followed by her two daughters, Miss Sophie and Miss Mary, together with Miss Jennie Swann, daughter of ex-Governor Swann of Maryland, and Miss Markoe, a sister of the present Colonel Frank Markoe of the 5th Maryland Regiment. And what a welcome it was! They all knew the disturbed condition of the country, and especially the condition of affairs in Baltimore, and insisted at once that I should make my stay at Cedar Park as long as possible. Under the circumstances, this was not hard to do, but it was hard to get away when once fixed there, particularly from such irresistible and charming young women.

Well, at breakfast, when the servants retired from the room (and those were good, old slave days in Maryland when the darkey knew his place, when it was the custom for the servants to retire after the breakfast had been placed upon the table), I soon informed them of my plans, and that in a few days I expected to gather together several young men in the neighbourhood and start for the South.

I was not long in securing recruits. Jim McCaleb, Harry Stuart, together with two young men, one by the name of Owens and the other Jones, and myself, formed a party of five. This was about the 5th or 6th of May. We arranged to start on our march the following night. Each of us possessed a good horse and a Colt 's revolver. By appointment we all met at our rendezvous, and rode away through Anne Arundel County until we reached the beautiful old home of Doctor Richard Stuart, historically known as Dodan, now, (as at time of first publication), the home of a Catholic sisterhood.

Doctor Stuart's family were rebels by inheritance, and there was no attempt to disguise this fact on the part of anyone. We all sat down to a glorious Maryland supper, and only left late in the evening with God's blessing upon our heads. We soon crossed the line of Anne Arundel into Prince George's and rode to the home of Captain John Contee, a retired U. S. Naval officer. It was with some difficulty that we rapped the old captain up at that hour of the night. He, however, put his head out of the window and we invited him down to meet us. He was a thorough Maryland gentleman of the old school, and before making any inquiry as to our plans and movements, he invited us to join him in a glass of whisky and water.

106

His beautiful daughter, Miss Florence, soon put in an appearance. It was just two o'clock in the morning, and in a few minutes we were again sitting down to a healthful repast of cold meat, cold bread and butter, pickles, whisky, milk, etc.

The captain had already asked us to take several drinks in the short space of fifteen minutes, and we were all fast getting into a happy frame of mind. When we told the captain we were going South, he said: "Gentlemen, you know I am a retired naval officer, and having served my country so long, I shall continue to uphold the flag. I would advise you young men to retrace your steps and return to your homes." Miss Florence held opposite views, and she was loud in her exclamations of praise that we were on our way to fight for the South.

I soon found we were tarrying too long, being too hospitably treated. We indulged again in the captain's good whisky, and when we mounted and said goodbye, we were prepared to oppose anything that came in our way.

The sun was rising on a bright May Sabbath morn as we rode into Laurel, a small village on the line of the Baltimore & Ohio Railroad.

Our itinerary directed us to take the road to Rockville, Montgomery County, but just outside of Laurel, and after having crossed the railroad track, we were met by a man driving a wagon, who informed us that a Yankee regiment had just encamped at Rockville about eight miles away, and that if it was our intention to pass through that town we had better scatter. It was very evident that we could not keep together, and after a short conference we decided that two would take the open country to the left, two the open country to the right, and that I should continue on the main road, going through the town, as originally designed, and join the others that evening at Claggett's Ford.

Just as I was entering the town of Rockville, I fancied I would escape the notice of the troops, but I had scarcely moved a step further when I saw several officers sitting on the fence on both sides of the road. There was nothing to do but to ride straight on. I passed through them and bowed graciously, when one of the officers cried, "Will you sell that horse?"

I was quite equal to the occasion, and replied, "Yes, I will on my return. I am on my way to pay a visit to Major Peters, who lives a few miles up the road. I expect to come back this way Wednesday, and will sell you the horse if you will give me $250 for him." Of course, I changed my mind and never came back. A fib, under such circumstances, was excusable.

I was not further molested, and after riding a couple of miles I reached Claggett's house, and from there was directed to Claggett's Ford. I was surprised to find my comrades already there, and as it was getting quite dark we arranged to spend the night in the culvert under the Chesapeake & Ohio Canal.

It was through this culvert that we were to reach the river in the morning, an unfrequented route across the Potomac. We had been advised that it was but seldom used.

We realized that we should have to sleep either on the banks of the river that night or under the culvert, when suddenly, to our great surprise, we heard a cry of a sentinel on the towpath "All's well". This went through us like a shot; it necessitated absolute silence on our part; so that we were obliged to stand by our horses' heads to prevent them from neighing.

It was a long and tiresome night, especially for young men who had had so little experience in such matters. The day was breaking when a question arose in our minds what to do with the sentinel. We must either shoot or capture him to avoid a general alarm before we crossed over the river. This question had to be decided at once, as the day was breaking rapidly. We made Jim McCaleb our captain, and he, being a resolute chap, ordered Harry Stuart to creep up the canal bank, with orders either to capture or kill the sentinel.

We waited some time in dread suspense, expecting every minute to hear the crack of Stuart's revolver, but not a sound was heard. Stuart finally crawled back into the culvert and said, "The pickets that we heard during the night have all been called in." Evidently they were on duty at night but relieved during the day. We were all very thankful to have matters take this shape, and no one was hurt. We should have deeply regretted taking the life of a soldier or picket under such circumstances.

There was no time to be lost. We were at once in the saddle, on the river's bank, into the water, plunging and swimming through rocks and holes, pressing on to the Virginia side.

In a few minutes more we safely landed. We got breakfast at a farmer's house, and afterwards he directed us on the road to Leesburg. We were wet to the skin. Without waiting to dry our clothes, and having no change with us, we pushed on.

On our arrival rooms were engaged at Pickett's hotel, and our horses were stabled for the night. We had fires made in our rooms and dried our clothes. In a short while we were in presentable shape.

We went out to see the sights and talk to the people. No introduction was needed. The fact that we were Marylanders and had come over to fight for Virginia gave us a hearty and hospitable welcome from all the citizens.

Leesburg was always noted for her pretty women, and we had a very pleasant evening with a great many of them. We were the recipients of much hospitality. Unfortunately the next day I fell sick, just as sick as I could be. I had evidently caught cold crossing the river, together with exposure to the heat, drinking and eating imprudently, doing everything in fact I ought not to have done, which resulted in a violent attack of dysentery. The country doctor was called in, and I was ordered immediately to bed to remain there until told by him to get up.

That very night, about midnight, cries were heard in the streets, people rushing to and fro and great excitement prevailing everywhere. The report had come into the town that the Yankees had crossed the Potomac at Edwards's Ferry in large force, and that a company of Maryland cavalry, commanded by Captain Gaither, then picketed at that point, were being rapidly driven in, and were retreating on the town. This, of course, started a panic in Leesburg. The houses were deserted, the hotel abandoned, the stables emptied, and no one remained with me but my faithful friend McCaleb, who declared he would not desert me no matter what happened. He came into my room and sat down by my side, both of us momentarily expecting the Yankees to enter the room. Hour after hour we waited without closing our eyes.

It proved a false alarm. The next morning I said to McCaleb: "Jim, I think with a little breakfast, I should feel better, and perhaps later in the day we could start on our way to join Ashby's cavalry. Go downstairs, old fellow, and see if our horses have been fed, and send me up some breakfast." McCaleb was not long gone. I could see by his expression that there was something to worry him more than Yankees. Almost breathless, he exclaimed, "Our horses have been stolen; there is no food in the kitchen and nothing for breakfast." I really felt like giving up the ghost, to lose that splendid horse of mine, for which I had so recently given $250 in gold, which money I had been a long time accumulating. It was enough to break a young cavalier's heart, to see his ambition shattered in this way. This noble charger was stolen from the stable that night by some comrade or Confederate, and I have never, from that day to this, found a trace of him.

All my plans and hopes to join Ashby's command were at an end. As I had no money excepting a few dollars left in my pocket and was weak and sick, McCaleb and I were sorely perplexed to determine what was next best to do; our disappointment was so keen that we almost cried. We knew that we should make cavalry soldiers, because we had been accustomed from our early youth to ride all kinds of horses, and we felt that under Ashby we should soon make records for ourselves.

But, as already stated, we were nearly out of money, had no one to vouch for us in any way, and there was nothing left to do but to buy a ticket to Richmond, and join the Maryland Infantry then organizing at that point.

CHAPTER 2

The First Maryland Confederate Regiment

We had to take a rather circuitous route in those days to reach Richmond,—by stage from Leesburg to Warrenton, a distance of forty miles, and by rail from Warrenton to Richmond.

On our arrival at Richmond, we put up at the Spottswood Hotel. Here I found a large number of Marylanders as undecided as ourselves as to what command they would join.

Captain William H. Murray, formerly connected with the Maryland Guard in Baltimore, was at Camp Lee recruiting. This company was being made up entirely of Marylanders. Captain Murray was eminently qualified to command the company. He was a good tactician, had been connected with the Guard in Baltimore for some years, and with the material he would gather around him there was no question but that he would organise a notable command.

I must not forget to say that my dear friend McCaleb left me at this time, and we never met again. He went to the far South to visit relatives, afterwards joined the Texas army, and was shot in one of the Trans-Mississippi battles.

There was nothing left for me to do but to join Murray's Company, which I did, and was duly enlisted into the Confederate service on May 17, 1861, to serve one year. We had daily drills and exercises until the Company was fully organized.

We were then ordered to Winchester, Va., to meet other Maryland companies, forming at different points to make up the First Maryland Confederate Regiment. Col. Arnold Elzey, of the old army, was with us at Camp Lee, and it was understood that he should command the regiment then organizing.

Captain George H. Steuart, a gallant son of Maryland, a graduate of West Point as well as a young officer who had seen considerable service in fighting the Indians, was to be our lieut.-colonel. Bradley T. Johnson, of Frederick, a young lawyer, was to be the major. Probably there was no regiment in the service that started out under brighter auspices or with better officer than the First Maryland.

The different companies came together at Winchester and were mustered into service to serve for twelve months. It made very little difference to the men who were to command them, provided the officers were all Marylanders.

We can all say with much pride that Elzey, Steuart and Johnson maintained throughout the war the highest distinction for bravery and soldierly conduct. Elzey and Steuart rose to be Major-Generals, and Johnson, although only a civilian, soon rose with distinction to the rank of brigadier-general. His military career was phenomenal, and to have had Lee, Joe Johnston and Jackson compliment him on the field was no small honour; he was recognized as a soldier most gallant and distinguished in the service of the South.

The 1st Maryland was put into a brigade composed of the 3rd Tennessee, the 13th Virginia and the 10th Virginia, under command of General Kirby Smith.

General Patterson, commanding the Federal forces, was organizing an army in the vicinity of Hagerstown, and was reported to have crossed the Potomac near Falling Waters, and to be marching toward Bunker Hill to engage our little army.

Col. Jackson, afterwards known as "Stonewall," was sent forward to reconnoitre and report Patterson's position. Jackson simply felt the enemy, capturing only a few prisoners, and no decisive engagement took place. He accomplished, however, the object of his mission, which gave General Johnston an insight into Patterson's whereabouts, and no doubt other valuable information in regard to the strength of his army.

We had already moved up ten miles north of Winchester to a small village named Darkesville. Here we celebrated the 4th of July, '61. We were drawn up in line of battle, expecting Patterson to come out and give us fight.

It was on this day that I remember having received the first letters from home, one from my dear mother and another from my aunt. My mother's letter was terribly sad, a message from a heart-broken woman. My aunt, who had bitterly opposed my going South and taking up arms against the Union, was not long in changing her views and her opinion of the question before the country. In her letter to me she said:

My nephew, I honour you for your self-sacrifice.

General Johnston rode down the line of battle on the Fourth of July, and stopping in front of our regiment said to Col. Elzey, "If your men fight as well as they yell, I expect good service of them." We remained in line of battle for several days, but each day Patterson declined to fight. It was hard and most depressing to stand out in the broiling sun without shelter of any kind, waiting for a clash with the enemy. We held a good position and were anxious to have Patterson attack us.

General Patterson displayed more military ability than we had given him credit for. Instead of attacking us in front, he made a detour to the left, and tried to outflank us. Johnston was on the alert and fell back toward Winchester, again taking up his original position, which was stronger and nearer our base of supplies.

We were kept busy in throwing up breastworks and mounting heavy guns, which was all good training, besides picketing on the outposts.

These experiences were rapidly forming us into good, raw troops and preparing us for the great conflict so near at hand, but which we little dreamed of.

On the 17th of July orders were received to break camp and prepare to march. As is the case with all raw troops, they think they know as much as their commanders, and if orders don't suit them, they are not inclined to obey them. There was quite a disposition to mutiny throughout the army when the different regiments moved into the turnpike, to find that the order was to march to the right instead of to the left. To march to the right was to march away from the enemy, and at the moment it looked like a further retreat.

We were not long in suspense. A general order was read to the army that General Beauregard,[1] at Manassas, was threatened by an overwhelming force of the enemy under General McDowell, and we were marching to his support, and every soldier was instructed to step out. This settled the question at once. I never saw men march before

---

1. *The Art of War*, two classic works on the attainment of victory, (*The Art of War* by Sun-Tzu and *Maxims of the Art of War* by Pierre G. T. Beauregard) also published by Leonaur.

or since the war with such alacrity. Every soldier was in his place; not a laggard in the line. So we pressed on to the Shenandoah, marching all night long and reaching the river at early dawn.

We went into the river, up to our necks, with our guns and ammunition raised over our heads, and the current was so swift that some of us locked arms to support each other. I remember that Southgate Lemmon and Tom Levering, my comrades, helped me across the river, and their assistance was very needful, otherwise I might have gone down. The march continued with wet clothes through Upperville to Piedmont Station, on the Manassas Gap Railroad. We encamped along the line of the road late Saturday night, July 20th, 1861.

McDowell's army at Centreville, moving on Manassas, took position for the battle the following day. We were all eager for a fight. Every man was in position, and all orders were cheerfully obeyed. We slept a little that night, but before 3 a. m. Sunday we were up and crowding into cars for a trip to the plains of Manassas. Our regiment, in fact our brigade, was the last to leave.

The fight had already begun. We could hear the cannon roar. The train which conveyed us stopped within three miles of Manassas Junction, about 1 o'clock on that hot Sabbath day.

The line was immediately formed, and a rapid march began in a northwesterly direction, to be in touch with the extreme left of our line. The heat was intense. Through ploughed fields and dusty roads we marched. No doubt the enemy was made aware of our coming in this way. As we came near the order was given to "double quick."

General Smith said: "Boys, if you double quick, you will still have a chance to get in the fight." We knew that we were nearing the battlefield, as the dead and wounded could be seen and heard on each side of us. Many said we were whipped; others said, "Go in boys, give them hell."

The arrival of Kirby Smith's brigade was most timely. Jackson had been wounded. Bee and Bartow fighting at the head of their regiments against desperate odds, had fallen dead at their posts. General Smith repeated the command "Step lively, boys, and we will be in time yet for a fight." So on we swept, cheer after cheer, marching with the thermometer at nearly 105, no water, tongues parched with red clay, when we came to a little stream where horses had fallen dead during the day; the water was already coloured with blood, but we sipped it up as a refreshing beverage.

We were moved up rapidly. It was just at this point that the first bullet from the enemy shot a member of Company C, John Berryman. The shot was fired from a regiment of Brooklyn Zouaves, that, under cover, fired a volley into us, wounding several men, but, comparatively speaking, doing but little damage. We here formed into line and returned this fire, driving the enemy from cover. General Smith was in the act of forming his brigade into line of battle when he was shot and fell from his horse. This was the first real live soldier that I had seen shot and fall from a horse, and of course I thought he was dead. He lived, however, to achieve an enviable reputation as a soldier, as well as a distinguished citizen and educator of the young men of the South.

Col. Elzey, the senior colonel, took command of the brigade. We moved on, steadily feeling the enemy in our front. We were ordered to lie down for a moment, until the artillery, under Lieut. Beckham, could take position on our left.

The artillery, concealed in the woods, opened a rapid and effective fire, creating havoc and confusion, when the order came for us to fix bayonets and charge. The enemy's line of battle, the extreme right of the Federal army, held quite a good position, well placed on the crest of a hill. We could see the colour-bearer waving the star-spangled banner, and the enemy apparently eager for a fight. Then the order came again to us to charge, and charge we did, straight up the hill in the face of the enemy. It surprised me very much that those fellows should have fired over our heads and wounded so few of us. In a moment more we had broken their lines and captured many prisoners.

The colour-bearer just referred to, poor fellow, was shot, and as we passed over his body we saw that he had entwined himself in the American flag. Our men, one and all, had a kind word for the gallant soldier. I think he came from the State of Maine. His regiment, in my opinion could have stayed there a little longer. Changing our front obliquely to the right, we could see the enemy in full retreat. There is no question but that the timely arrival of Kirby Smith's brigade had a most important influence in determining the result of that day, and General Smith goes down in history as the Blucher.

It was getting late in the afternoon, and no orders to pursue the enemy had been received. Colonel Elzey moved a portion of the brigade, including our regiment, to a point where the fight had been hottest, and where we saw two regular batteries of artillery completely annihilated, horses and men lying piled up dead and no one left but an old cannoneer, still standing by his gun ready to load. It was just at this point that Beauregard rode up and promoted Elzey on the field to be a brigadier-general. I have participated in and seen a great many battles since that fight, especially Cold Harbor, Gettysburg, Spotsylvania, and I might mention others, but for a short distance along the line, the slaughter of the enemy was as appalling as anything I witnessed during the war.

The fighting had been terrific in front of Jackson, and down Bee's and Bartow's lines. The contending forces along this position had, on several occasions during the day, crossed bayonets. McHenry Howard and I tried to do something to alleviate the sufferings of the wounded. I remember offering my canteen to some of the poor Federals and was surprised to find that their minds were so poisoned against Southerners as to think we desired to give them poison to drink. It was necessary to drink the water from the canteen first myself before I could restore confidence in these dying men, and then they gasped, "Thank God, thank God!"

We went into camp several miles from the stone bridge. It had been a hard and rough day. We had had nothing to eat, and no rations were issued until noon of the next day; but we all sank down to rest that night with thankful hearts that death had not come to us.

It was our first battle, and although our regiment had not been hotly engaged at any time, still its behaviour had been such as to establish a mutual confidence of man to man that the right stuff was there, and we should be heard from whenever the occasion required.

From this time until the following spring there were no battles fought; it was mere routine camp duty with occasional skirmishes on the picket-line. I shall not attempt to describe the experiences of camp life and other events incident to the life of a private soldier during this period.

CHAPTER 3

Sickness

The early autumn of 1861 was spent in the vicinity of Fairfax C.H. With no enemy near, many of the soldiers were permitted to visit the farmers' and officers' houses, and in this way we formed very pleasant acquaintances and associations. The life, however, was saddened by the sanitary condition of the army. In fact, the whole army was infected with all manner of diseases—fever, measles, whooping-cough, but particularly typhoid fever.

I think it was in the early part of September that I was stricken down with typhoid fever. I was ill for more than nine weeks. Most of the time I lay on the hard ground, receiving very little attention from anybody. My life was almost despaired of, and no doubt I should have died but for a providential occurrence.

I asked my doctor one morning what were my chances of recovery, and his reply was not cheerful. I said to him, "Doctor, if you will only take me to a house, strip me of these vile clothes filled with vermin and put me in a clean bed, I shall live." The Lord was truly merciful to me, for on the very day of this conversation a messenger, as it were, arrived in the form of a gentleman from Fauquier County, Virginia, who came in his carriage to take a few of the sick soldiers to his home.

He said he had come specially to look after the sick Marylanders, who had no homes in his country, and the doctor and officers of my company singled me out as one of the sickest in the camp. I was put on a couch and carried by four faithful comrades to the station, and from there conveyed in an open freight car some thirty miles to Piedmont Station on the Manassas Gap Railroad.

I reached there late in the afternoon to find an ox-cart with a mattress in the bottom, to carry me to Bollingbrook, the beautiful estate of Mr. Robert Bolling, of Fauquier County, Va. The old ox-cart, although it had a mattress, gave me a good jolting, as may be imagined, before arriving at his house.

In fact; I may say I was nearly dead when I got there. The good servants carried me in their arms to a room on the second floor. Here they stripped off the old clothes from my body, and with hot water and alcohol bathed my bed sores. I was almost a Lazarus. A nice clean night-shirt was put on, and a glass of old Port revived my waning spirits, and just before the tea-bell rang I found myself in a comfortable bed surrounded by genuine Virginia hospitality, and refined, sympathetic people who were ready to make every sacrifice for my comfort. I fell asleep that night without my usual dose of morphia, and it was a sweet sleep, for during the night the fever left me, and I awoke in the morning feeling that a change had come over me.

By careful nursing, day by day, I gradually grew better. The beautiful Miss Tabb Bolling, of Petersburg, Va., afterwards Mrs. Gen. Wm. F. H. Lee, and her cousin, Miss Anna Bolling, of Bollingbrook, were in constant attendance, and they did as much for me as a sister would do for a brother.

In the course of three weeks I was permitted to sit up, and a few days later I was taken down stairs for a comfortable seat on the porch. I was gaining strength rapidly, and looked forward to meeting my old comrades again in a few weeks.

Let me stop here to say a word. The men from Maryland, away from their homes, especially those who were sick (and most of them took their turn at it) owe an everlasting debt of gratitude to the women of Virginia. And what can we say about them? What splendid women they were! What self-sacrifices they endured, and with what heroism and courage they withstood the horrors of those terrible times!

I would mention here a long list of names of families kind to me during the war, but let a few suffice. The Bollings, McFarlands, Braxtons, Alexanders, Stephensons, Pendletons, Buchanans, Dandridges, and Washingtons were only a few of the noble families to whom I owe a lasting gratitude, and whom I hope never to forget.

I remained at Bollingbrook until late in November and then bade adieu to those charming surroundings, to return to my regiment encamped at Manassas Junction. How pleasant it was to see the faces of my old comrades again! There was Gres Hough, Nick Watkins, Sam Sindall, Frank Markoe, South Lemmon and others, whose names at the moment I cannot recall. They all greeted me most affectionately.

They had built a very comfortable log hut for the winter, and were living the lives of real soldiers. I was soon at home and initiated into the mysteries of camp life once more. Several hours each day were devoted to camp exercises and drill, hunting wild turkeys, playing cards, and on Sunday some clergyman would come in and preach to the camp.

I vividly recall Bishop Johns, of Virginia. He was interested in all the young men, and particularly in those from Maryland, and the men of the regiment were always glad to see him and listen to the gospel story as told by him.

Here in winter quarters we were working hard preparing for the opening of the spring campaign of 1862.

CHAPTER 4

With Jackson

We broke camp at Manassas early in March, 1862, and retired to the Rappahannock River. Our brigade became now a part of Ewell's Division, Jackson's Corps, Army of Northern Virginia. The main army, under command of Gen. Joseph E. Johnston, continued its march towards Gordonsville, while our division remained on the Rappahannock.

The weather was simply wretched, so much so that it was most difficult, in fact next to an impossibility, for the army to move. Here we remained about six weeks, when finally we received orders to cross the Blue Ridge and report to General Jackson in the valley. General Jackson had about this time encountered the enemy at Kernstown, and while compelled to retire, he had made one of the most gallant fights of the war, overwhelmed as he was by superior numbers.

Our division halted at Conrad's Store in the Luray Valley. To our great surprise, Jackson had gone when we arrived. The old story is that Ewell sat on the fence and cried because no one could tell him of Jackson's whereabouts. We could get no tidings of Jackson; no one knew where to find him; his camp had been abandoned, and all that was known was that he had moved rapidly in the direction of Staunton, Va.

Jackson had his plans, however, and was preparing to make another of his brilliant manoeuvres. A large Federal force under General Milroy was advancing towards McDowell in what is now West Virginia. This was a portion of Fremont's army, and Jackson, to carry out his plan of defeating Banks, at Winchester, must first destroy Milroy in Virginia. This movement was a success. He made a very rapid march, met the enemy and accomplished his purpose, retraced his steps as rapidly as possible and rejoined Gen. Ewell.

A part of Jackson's plan was to destroy Banks at Winchester, and carry out President Davis's and Gen. Johnston's scheme,—even if it involved the withdrawal of a large body of troops from the peninsula,—and reach the North by way of the Valley, striking a sudden and heavy blow at some exposed position, capturing Washington if possible.

These plans, however, never fully materialised. After the battle of McDowell, where the enemy had been repulsed at every point, and Jackson had driven them sufficiently to the rear to cover his own movement, he pressed on down the valley.

General Banks retired as rapidly as possible to Winchester, where the principal engagement of the campaign took place, resulting ultimately in a complete overthrow of the occupation of the Valley of Virginia by Northern troops.

General Ewell moved from Conrad's Store to Front Royal, and Jackson from Harrisonburg to the same place. This movement began on May 18, 1862. As Ewell's Division approached Front Royal, General Ewell was informed by the citizens that Col. Kenly, a Marylander, commanding about 1,000 Marylanders, with a battery of artillery, was in command at that point.

Our regiment that morning was bringing up the rear of Ewell's Division, when Gen. Ewell transmitted an order to Bradley T. Johnson, that it had been reported to him that the enemy in his front were Marylanders, and if we wished to meet Marylanders, to move our regiment to the front at once.

The challenge was accepted immediately, and the whole army halted that we might take the front skirmish line, which position we held throughout the fight, and finally routed the enemy, our fellow citizens from Maryland.

I forgot to mention that about this time the first year's service of the Maryland regiment had expired, and the men were entitled to an honourable discharge with privilege of re-enlisting, or entering other branches of the service.

We were mustered out on the 17th day of May in accordance with law, but to the credit of the men be it stated that every man took his old place in the ranks, to participate in the glorious succession of victories which were to crown Jackson's campaign.

The first fight took place at Front Royal, the 1st Maryland leading the advance of Ewell's division. Colonel Kenly made a good fight and displayed conspicuous gallantry in the field, but he was over-matched. His conduct was the admiration of every soldier. He was captured with more than 600 prisoners. The last stand was made at the bridge over the Shenandoah River, and I distinctly recall one poor fellow who fell dead just as he turned to cross the bridge. He was in my immediate front. We were double-quicking and firing at the same time. I am not positive who killed him; I am glad I am not able to say; bullets were flying thick and fast. He was a well-dressed officer, and as I came up to his dead body I could not resist relieving him of a long pair of cavalry boots which he wore. The temptation was too great and I could not let someone else make this important capture. I stooped down and relieved him of them, and found them to be of great service for months and months after, and especially when I joined the cavalry a few weeks later.

Jackson and Ewell pressed on to Winchester. We were getting a good taste of Jackson's foot cavalry at that time, marching from 20 to 30 miles a day, and frequently without food of any kind.

As is usual after typhoid fever, one grows fat; my weight reached 180 pounds, but after the valley campaign, and marching some five or six hundred miles in forty days. I settled down to 136 pounds. I was never in better health or better fighting trim in my life.

Just before the Battle of Winchester, Jackson called on Ewell for our brigade. We were placed under Jackson's immediate command on the extreme left. The other two brigades of Ewell's Division had gone into action on the right.

We were held in reserve until the battle was well under way, when Elzey moved, left in rear, to turn, if possible, the enemy's right.

General Gordon, of the Federal army, was in immediate command of Banks's forces in our front, and he must have been a soldier of some skill as he anticipated this movement and prevented the success which we had hoped for. They fired upon us at close range, but it did not check our advance.

Then it was that Dick Taylor, commanding the gallant Louisianans, rose suddenly from cover just to our right and the two brigades swept irresistibly forward, the Yankees giving way at every point. Jackson urged his men to press on to the Potomac, and our brigade led in the pursuit. The Northern troops were falling in every direction. The fruits of this victory, however, were lost, excepting the enormous supplies captured in Winchester, owing to the lack of disciplined cavalry. If Jackson had had cavalry, the entire army of Banks would have been captured before they reached the Potomac River. After the battle one almost seemed compensated for risking his life, especially on an occasion like the taking of Winchester, to see the people hail us as their deliverers. They were almost frantic with joy, and it is said that General Jackson smiled and asked a lady, "Who's been here since I've been gone?"

We were all too tired to push the enemy and therefore they escaped to the Potomac. Next morning, however, we continued our march to Halltown, on the direct road to Harper's Ferry.

The afternoon of the day following we stormed Bolivar Heights, Gen. George H. Steuart being in command. This stronghold was held by a Yankee regiment, who were just sitting down to a sumptuous repast when we drove in their pickets, creating such confusion that the tables were all left spread with the supper untouched, so that we could sit down to finish it ourselves.

That regiment could have made a gallant defines, but for some reason they "skedaddled" at the sight of a rebel. We heartily enjoyed their supper. We captured a great many guns and much ammunition without the loss of a single man. That night we slept on the roadside with our faces towards Winchester.

The order came before daybreak to march. We marched the entire day, through Winchester and Middletown on the road to Strasburg up to 10 o'clock that night, covering a distance of 35 miles, and when we rested, we rested without food and with fence-rails for our pillows.

Fortunately the wagons came up in the night and rations were issued at 5 o'clock the following morning. We were soon again on the march, *en route* for Strasburg. We poor privates knew very little of the danger that surrounded us. We afterwards learned that it was just touch and go whether or not the enemy had entrapped Jackson.

Shields had crossed the Blue Ridge Mountain on the east, and marched from Front Royal towards Strasburg. Fremont was coming on from the west towards Wardensville on our right, and Banks, having learned of our retrograde movement, had recrossed the Potomac, and, as he supposed, in conjunction with Shields, Milroy and Fremont, Jackson would be gobbled up, but the plan failed for lack of co-operation, and nobody knew better than Jackson how to take advantage of it.

In another day our army was safe; the combined forces of the Federal army were in our rear. We had marched 170 miles in eleven days, and engaged in two battles, Front Royal and Winchester, threatened on all sides by an army of 60,000 against 15,000 under Jackson. We whipped the enemy in detail, and triumphantly escaped from them without losing a single wagon.

Jackson moved slowly up the valley. His men were tired; they needed rest and food; but he was eternally vigilant awaiting an opportunity to fight. Quite a little skirmish occurred on June 6th, a few miles east of Harrisonburg. General Fremont had sent Percy Wyndham, with a large force of infantry and cavalry, to harass our rear. They met Colonel Turner Ashby, supported by the 58th Virginia Regiment. Ashby had been sent out to check any further advance. A severe fight ensued. Our line wavered, and Ashby, appealing to his men to charge, fell pierced through the heart, and in a moment everything was in confusion.

It was just then that the 1st Maryland, under Col. Bradley T. Johnson, came up in time to save the day. Col. Johnson gave the order to charge, and it was a charge that those who participated in it will never forget. Johnson led us to victory. We were close to the fire of the enemy, it being quite late in the evening, but this did not deter us. On went our regiment until it had routed the crack Pennsylvania Bucktails, capturing 287 prisoners, including Colonel Kane, their commander. We avenged the death of Ashby. This was really the first good fight of our regiment.

We saw many of our comrades fall, but the conduct of the men was simply superb, and General Ewell ordered that we should wear on our colours one of the captured "bucktails" as a trophy.

The next day Gen. Ewell issued a general order, saying that it was due to the intrepid conduct of the 1st Maryland Regiment that the death of Ashby had been avenged. I shall never forget that night: it was one of the saddest of the war. My friend Sam Sindall had been shot while resting his head on my knee just before we were ordered to charge.

Two days later we fought the battle of Cross Keys. Our company were deployed as skirmishers. I was on the advance line for more than six hours, constantly under fire.

We had issued to us 128 rounds of ammunition, and when the fighting in the evening ended we had scarcely a cartridge left. We witnessed the fall of several of our best young men. McKenny White and Willie Colston were desperately wounded, and at the time there seemed little hope for their recovery, but they both survived, the latter meeting a soldier's death at a later period.

Gen. George H. Steuart received a grape shot in the shoulder, which disabled him for nearly six months. I received a slight scratch on the right cheek from a glancing ball, which practically paralyzed my face for some weeks. The next day my cheek was perfectly black. I was struck just as I turned to pick up Lieut. Bean, of Company I, who had been standing immediately in my rear and was wounded in the foot. I had advised him the moment before to get away as he would certainly be struck, but he was a gallant fellow, and did not heed the warning.

I suffered from considerable nausea, produced by this nervous shock, which continued the following day, and I was excused by my captain from marching with the company; on this account I was not engaged in the Battle of Port Republic.

This was the last infantry fight in which I should have taken part. The next day our company went out of service, many of them receiving staff appointments, some re-enlisting in the 2nd Maryland Infantry, while others, like myself, joined the cavalry.

I had served more than a year in the infantry.

CHAPTER 5

The Maryland Cavalry

After the discharge from Murray's company, we marched with the army to Gordonsville, and there I joined Company A, Maryland Cavalry, Captain Ridgely Brown in command, First Lieutenant Frank A. Bond, Second Lieutenant Thomas Griffith, Third Lieutenant Ventris Pue.

I secured a few days leave of absence, and went by train to Staunton to buy a horse. Succeeding in this, I returned at once to Gordonsville. It would have been difficult indeed to have found a better cavalry organisation than the one commanded by Captain Brown.

The company was composed chiefly of men who had been in the infantry for a year, while quite a number of them had recently crossed the Potomac to espouse the cause of the South.

We were temporarily attached to the Second Virginia Cavalry, under Col, Thomas Munford, a gallant and distinguished Virginian, who was particularly proud of his Maryland company, so much so that he placed us as the first company on the right.

Here at Gordonsville General Jackson and his army were resting after the fatiguing Valley campaign. I was in camp, in the woods near General Jackson's headquarters, and while sitting on the fence one evening Captain Pendleton, of Jackson's staff, saw me and inquired if I should like to be detailed for courier duty. We had been old friends at the University of Virginia before the war, and Pendleton said: "Come over to Jackson's headquarters and report for courier duty." With the consent of my captain, I soon got ready.

General Jackson and staff were lodged in a large white farmhouse, with a wooden porch in front, just outside of Gordonsville, and as I rode up I recognized the general walking up and down the porch.

I told him that I had come to report to him for duty as a courier by order of Captain Pendleton, and was ready to receive any orders he might give me. I had never spoken to General Jackson before, although I had frequently seen him on the march and in the Valley.

General Jackson's first order directed me to go to each Brigade headquarters and deliver to each commanding officer positive instructions to move their respective commands that evening not later than 9 o'clock on the road to Louisa C. H., and when in line to await further orders.

I got back to headquarters about 10 o'clock. I had had some ten brigade commanders to interview, which was no easy task for a green courier like myself. I accomplished the work, however, and reported to General Jackson that the army was moving in accordance with his instructions. He turned to me and asked if I had had anything to eat. I answered that I had not, when he said, "Go downstairs in the dining-room of this house, and you will find my mess-chest. Get something out of it, and report to me at 5 o'clock in the morning."

I enjoyed a hearty supper, and after feeding my horse, fell asleep on the porch, but was aroused in time to be in the saddle at the hour designated.

From that time on, until after the great battles around Richmond, I was constantly in the saddle at the great general's side, and I feel that I at least rendered service quite equal, if not fully equal, to that of some of the members of his staff. I was with him on the march from Gordonsville to Louisa C. H., from Louisa C. H. to Hanover Junction, from Hanover Junction to Ashland, from Ashland on the road leading to Pole Green Church, endeavouring to form a line in touch with Hill's division, then about attacking the enemy at Mechanicsville.

Jackson's corps bore constantly to the left, turning Beaver Dam Creek, moving en echelon towards old Cold Harbor.

It was at the beginning of this engagement that I saw Jackson raise his hands to Heaven and pray for victory. Jackson hoped to strike the enemy in rear, and in conjunction with Hill, press him down the Chickahominy. Some confusion and delay prevented the success of this movement, and General Jackson has been criticised for undue delay in taking his proper position, but this question I shall not discuss, because I know he had almost insurmountable obstacles to overcome.

Jackson moved the next morning towards old Cold Harbor, supported by D. H. Hill's division on his right and Stuart's cavalry on his left. It was not until quite late in the afternoon, however, that Jackson, hearing the battle raging along Longstreet's and Hill's front, pressed in and hotly engaged the enemy.

Never before nor since have I witnessed such a scene. How I escaped being shot is still a mystery to me, and how my horse escaped is a still greater wonder. Jackson had me constantly "on the go," carrying orders in every direction under fire along the entire line in which Hill's and Ewell's divisions were engaged.

The fight continued into dark night, and the greatest confusion ensued. I heard someone say the following morning that Jackson and all of his staff had barely escaped capture.

When it was quite dark, we encountered the enemy's outpost in front of us, and Jackson made us charge and capture the post of about twenty men.

We moved early the next morning towards Gaines's Mill, but owing to the destruction of a bridge, we were unable to arrive in time on that day to engage the enemy. Likewise, at the Battle of Frazier's farm, we were prevented by the same reason.

I had now been under fire almost constantly for five days. The Battle of Frazier's farm occurred on the sixth day. The next morning I was more than gratified to see Colonel Munford, the colonel of my regiment, report for duty to General Jackson. They had just arrived from the valley to rejoin the army.

I asked Captain Pendleton to permit me to return to my company, if my services were no longer needed. The request was granted, and thus I escaped the great and terrible clash of arms which took place the next morning at Malvern Hill.

I had had enough of it for a time at least. Things did not look very pleasant for me around headquarters. General Jackson had been in a bad humour for several days; the truth of the matter is that he and his men had been completely worn out by what they had gone through.

In this battle the Confederates lost 20,000 men; Jackson's corps almost half that number, and no wonder he was troubled and mortified that, after so great a sacrifice, the enemy had escaped.

CHAPTER 6

2nd Virginia Cavalry

The past year had been an extremely eventful period in my life. It was a good thing to be thrown back on one's own resources. I began to grow serious. How I escaped being killed or wounded during the recent terrific campaign has always been a wonder to me. I owe my life to a merciful Providence.

I ascribe a great deal of my success in after life to the hardships and privations endured during the Civil War. Hardships set the mind free to discover, invent and plan.

I professed my faith in God early in life, but I have never felt as though I were a good man, free from shortcomings and frivolities. After all the miraculous escapes during the war, every soldier should try to love God, and try to be the kind of man God would have him to be. I remember distinctly that I soliloquized upon all this just after those terrible seven days' battles around Richmond. They set me to thinking; I was a much better soldier after that experience.

There was great rejoicing in Richmond and throughout the South after the defeat of McClellan, and after the safety of the Capital had been assured.

Our regiment, the Second Virginia Cavalry, did not tarry near Richmond long. We were ordered to join Jackson's forces, a portion of which had already arrived at Gordonsville. This was just preceding the battle of Cedar Mountain.

I cannot recall all that occurred in the early part of this campaign. I did not actively participate in this battle beyond the usual picket and flank duty. I knew that Jackson was preparing to force Pope's army across the Rappahannock, and no doubt there would be another great battle fought when General Lee came up with his main army.

The cavalry, under Jeb Stuart, was harassing Pope's right flank. At midnight, one dark, stormy night, we captured Pope's headquarters at Catlett's Station. This was a great ride. The streams were overflowing their banks. We approached the station from the direction of Warrenton while it was raining hard, and the men were drenched to the skin. It was just the weather for such sport. We swam two streams and reached the coveted spot about midnight.

The camp was surprised by a dashing charge, and the entire command, numbering about 300 prisoners, captured.

We were very much amused the next morning to see one of the men attired in General Pope's full-dress uniform. Pope himself escaped only because he happened to be away that night.

I have a very indistinct recollection of what occurred the following day. I know, however, that we were moving in the direction of Manassas Junction, and Jackson's corps was pressing on to get in Pope's rear, while the cavalry marched between, protecting Jackson's right flank.

The object of the movement was, if possible, to cut off Pope and capture the vast supplies which had been accumulated at Manassas Junction.

During the two or three days before the great battle of Second Bull Run was fought, we were constantly engaged in skirmishing and harassing the enemy.

Colonel Henderson, in the *Life of Jackson*, described the cavalry fight which took place on the afternoon of the 30th of August as probably the most brilliant sabre charge in the war.

My company, commanded by Capt. Ridgely Brown,—first company in front, Second Virginia Cavalry, Army of Northern Virginia,—was Ordered to reconnoitre and report.

General Lee was already pressing Pope's army, and Stuart's cavalry was stationed on the extreme right, ready to take advantage of any opportunity to charge the retreating enemy. We were not long in sending back word to Colonel Munford that several regiments of Federal cavalry were in our immediate front. Colonel Munford and his regiment came up at a dashing gait, forming front into line, our company on the right.

Colonel Broadhead, commanding the Sixth Michigan Cavalry, moved out to take the same position just in front of us. Here stood the two opposing regiments, within one hundred yards of each other, face to face. The excitement was intense. We were ordered to fight with sabres, and the command, "Draw sabres, forward, trot, gallop, charge!" rang out from both commanders.

Colonel Broadhead was killed and Colonel Munford received a sabre cut over the head. The two regiments locked sabres. Almost immediately support from both sides dashed into the fight. The dust and confusion became so great as to make it almost impossible to distinguish friend from foe.

I had joined the cavalry only a few weeks before, and it was my first cavalry fight. Unfortunately for me, my sabre, a poor specimen of Confederate iron, was soon bent and quite useless. I was attacked by three Yankees. I was fighting for my life, when kindly aid came from one of my comrades by the name of Nelson, who cut down two of my opponents, and at the third I made a right cut which missed him, and which nearly unhorsed me. Scarcely recovering my seat, I saw an officer coming straight at me tierce-point.

I had only a moment to gather my thoughts, and in that moment my pistol was levelled at him, to surrender or die. He threw up his hands and surrendered—horse, foot and dragoon. He was an officer of one of the Michigan cavalry regiments. During the remainder of the war I rode in his saddle. His sabre I presented to my cousin, Capt. James Shaw Franklin, of the Second Maryland Infantry.

I may here tell a story on my old friend. Bob Keene. His horse ran away in the charge, and it was not until late that night that he found his way back to camp, without horse, sword or hat, and said that, to escape being captured, he had crawled into a hollow tree, and had remained there until everything was quiet.

Every word of this was true, for Bob Keene was a brave fellow, and it was not fear of the enemy that put him in this plight.

The following day Colonel Munford's regiment moved to Leesburg. As soon as we got there we engaged the enemy in the streets. Meem's Partisan Rangers, numbering six hundred men, were routed and most of them captured. I was fortunate in capturing a live Yankee and a good horse, ridding myself of the old scrub which I had purchased a few months before while at Staunton, Va.

I was now well mounted and well equipped with Yankee sabre, Yankee saddle, Yankee boots and Yankee horse, ready for the Maryland campaign of 1862.

Gen. Fitz Lee, in command of the Confederate cavalry, preceded the army into Maryland. My company was still attached to the Second Virginia. We crossed the river at Edwards's Ferry, marching in the direction of Frederick City, taking up position in a little town called Urbana.

We were to guard General Lee's right flank against any sudden attack of the enemy approaching from the direction of Washington.

Lee was concentrating his army in the vicinity of Frederick City, moving on the road to Boonesboro' and Hagerstown, and crossing South Mountain at Crampton's Gap. Lee had sent Jackson by Turner's Gap to capture Harper's Ferry, which was accomplished in fine style.

Our company was still attached to Munford's regiment, bringing up the rear of Lee's army. We all enjoyed the kindly reception received from the citizens of Frederick. They were hospitable and liberal in their donations of good things.

Up to this time we had not been pressed by the enemy. In passing through Crampton's Gap, however, the Yankee cavalry overtook our regiment. They greatly outnumbered us; in fact, they were supported by Franklin's division of infantry, and soon drove us from our position. We suffered severely in this fight. Lee's army was forming on the west bank of Antietam Creek, awaiting the return of Jackson. McClellan moved cautiously when he should have moved with great rapidity. Finally there ensued one of the most sanguinary and bloody battles of the war,—the Battle of Antietam.

Our command in this fight occupied a position to the extreme right of the army, and while we witnessed a stubbornly contested struggle for two days, we were not actively engaged ourselves. We could, however, see the desperate fighting going on on both sides, without being exposed to it.

Our army retired across the Potomac without being further molested by the enemy. On this march our company brought up the rear.

CHAPTER 7

1st Maryland Batallion of Cavalry

On returning to Virginia we were ordered to take position near Snicker's Ferry, on the Shenandoah River, We picketed for some weeks on the river.

Major Charles Lewis lived nearby, and, with his charming wife, entertained us most hospitably for the few weeks we were in the vicinity of the old Shenandoah Springs, quite a noted place in days gone by.

Here we were enabled to give our horses a much needed rest, and we amused ourselves, when not on picket duty, by shooting partridges and different kinds of game.

We were ordered from this point to Leesburg, and arrived there one Sunday evening at dark. The girls were delighted to see this splendid regiment of Virginians and Marylanders, and ran out of their houses to kiss our horses, but I will not say how many of the men kissed the girls.

Capt. Frank A. Bond, in a recent letter to me, recalls the fact that my mess had a lot of pies made of preserves. We had ordered more pies than we could eat, and as we had to break camp the following morning, we invited the officers to participate in our frugal repast. It was just at this time that I met with a very serious loss. My horse, which I valued very highly, developed a fistula, and I had to leave him to his fate. No one except a cavalryman knows how deeply one becomes attached to his animal, which has carried him safely through so many perilous and dangerous encounters in war.

I abandoned him in a good field of grass, and I hope he finally got well, to render to someone else the same good service that he had done to me.

We were now getting into the autumn months, beautiful October, and our company was encamped at Winchester, under command of

Gen. George H. Steuart, who was subsequently relieved by Gen. William E. Jones.

For the past three months we had been the first company in front of the Second Virginia Cavalry, and during this time we had achieved a reputation quite enviable in the army. Colonel Munford had frequently applauded our company for its conduct in battle, and we were loath to part from such good friends.

There were, however, several Maryland companies organizing for the purpose of forming the First Maryland Battalion of Cavalry, and three of them came together at Winchester for this purpose, and elected our Captain, Ridgely Brown, major of the battalion.

The weather continued beautiful, and we remained a while longer in the neighbourhood of Winchester, picketing on the Romney road, at the gap in the mountains several miles away. Here we could get fine pheasant shooting, and in this way amused ourselves before going into winter quarters. After the first of December we moved up the valley near Edenburg.

Here another company joined the battalion, and we went into permanent winter quarters. We had daily drills, and improvised a race-track. We had many exciting races, at other times played cards, etc.

On one occasion two of my comrades, Gustav Lurman and Charlie Inloes, introduced a "*vingt-et-un* bank." The men were flush, having just been paid off. I had never seen the game played, but after watching it for a short time, I concluded to take a hand. I was most successful in all my ventures, winning upwards of $1,200 in Confederate money, which broke the bank for the time being. The next morning, however, additional capital was secured, and the game started afresh, although I was not permitted to play, as they were afraid of my good luck.

On January 2nd, 1863, a bitter cold day, the whole brigade started on an expedition to Moorefield, marching all day and all night, crossing the mountains. Many men were frostbitten. Both of my heels were badly nipped, but I soon recovered. We had expected to encounter the enemy near Moorefield. The suffering of the men was intense, and General Jones became very unpopular for this movement.

On February 23rd, our company, under command of Captain Bond, was informed by one of Jones' scouts that a company of Yankee cavalry, picketing near Winchester, could be easily captured.

An expedition was made up, and we started on a cold, chilly afternoon, reckoning to reach the outlying pickets about midnight. Led by a faithful guide, we arrived at the expected time, and succeeded in working our way to the rear of the command, resulting in the capture of the entire Yankee company.

Accomplishing this, we started at a trot to get away with our prisoners. We felt sure the enemy would pursue, and, as expected, they were soon on our track. We quickened our pace from trot to gallop. Captain Bond, with the usual foresight of a good officer, dispatched two of his men to inform General Jones that one or two regiments were closing in on us, and to be ready to meet them when we came up.

We were in no condition to fight after a gallop of nearly eighty-seven miles. General Jones had promptly ordered the Seventh Cavalry to mount, and before we reached New Market they were moving down the turnpike, nicely closed up and ready for the charge. This was fun for the Virginians.

Those who had been pursuing us through the night, without due regard to the risk of being attacked, had strung themselves out for miles along the pike, and the Virginians, coming out fresh and well closed up, soon made havoc among them, capturing, wounding and killing three hundred men.

It was a most successful raid on our part, and Captain Bond was complimented for the manner in which he had handled the expedition.

It was while I was in winter quarters that I had the pleasure of making the acquaintance of Capt. George Blackford, one of Lee's most noted scouts, who was temporarily assigned to duty in the Valley of Virginia.

Captain Blackford invited me to accompany him on a little expedition down the valley, to capture a wagon-train of the enemy, which was in the habit of passing daily between Winchester and Berryville. There were six of us in all, and we had been informed that five four-horse teams, with a quartermaster, drivers and an escort of three cavalrymen, generally composed the party, and would pass a given point about 2 o'clock in the afternoon.

On each side of the turnpike between Winchester and Berryville, where it crosses the Opequon, the banks were very high. It was at this point that we concluded to make the attack. Our horses were securely tied in the woods, thirty or forty yards in our rear, and we crawled up to the crest of the hill, and, peeping over the banks, waited for the approach of the wagon-train.

We were not long in suspense. Captain Blackford had ordered three of us to fall upon the enemy in front, and three in rear, with cocked revolvers, and to shoot immediately if we met with any resistance.

We captured the whole train. Each Yankee driver was ordered to lead out his team and three cavalrymen to dismount. A side road was within fifty yards of us, where we had tied our horses, and the whole party was away in a jiffy.

The wagons, with the supplies, were abandoned. We could not attempt to carry them off over the rough roads. Our prize consisted in all of twenty-three horses and seven prisoners. We pressed on to Millwood and Front Royal that night, passing north under cover of the Massanutton Mountain. We reached New Market the following morning with our prisoners and horses.

A few days later Captain Blackford came into camp and handed me six hundred dollars in gold as my share of the proceeds of the sale of the horses. This was a privilege accorded to scouts and not to regular army officers and privates. Money of this kind I always sent to my banker in Richmond, to be applied equally for credit of my brother and myself, the former being in the infantry. This gave us plenty of money for some months to come, and enabled us to keep up a respectable outfit.

Shortly after this time, during the month of April, I was suddenly taken sick with a bilious attack, and could not go with my company on the West Virginia expedition to Greenland's Gap.

I spent most of the time in bed at Mrs. Thomas Jordan's house, in Luray, Va., and she was very kind and good to me. I soon recovered, however, and rejoined my company on its return to the valley, about the first of June, 1863.

We were detached at this point from the Maryland Battalion, and ordered to report to General Ewell as his bodyguard. The old brigade, under command of General Jones, had been ordered east of the Blue Ridge to join General Stuart's command in the vicinity of Culpeper C. H.

Gen. Robert E. Lee was evidently concentrating his whole army in this vicinity, some twenty miles south of Winchester, preparatory to another invasion of Maryland and Pennsylvania.

Milroy was at Winchester and Berryville, and Ewell was moving on Winchester with his corps. It took position for battle on the morning of June 14th, Early leading the attack. Johnson's Division had been moved north of Winchester that night to anticipate, if possible, any attempt of Milroy to escape towards Martinsburg, but Johnson could not reach his position in time to intercept Milroy. He got away with a small body of troops on the road to Harper's Ferry.

The next morning Winchester surrendered, leaving in our hands several thousand prisoners, and a large quantity of stores, cannon, wagons and horses. It was a complete destruction of Milroy's army.

To be assigned to duty at the headquarters of a general commanding a corps was quite an elevation for us. We anticipated pleasant military experiences, which were more than realised before we got through the Gettysburg campaign.

At Hagerstown, where a number of our men resided prior to the war, they met old friends and relatives, and were most royally treated. At Chambersburg and Carlisle, although in the enemy's country, we received many smiles from the girls peeping through the windows. No damage of any kind was done to property, and the citizens generally looked upon us as a rather civilized and well-behaved crowd.

Captain Bond was authorized by General Ewell to make occasional scouts in the vicinity, to replenish our larder or pick up something good for the boys. We invited ourselves one day to dine at a good-looking house, with big barns and well-stored granaries. We ventured to order a dinner for ten. At first the old lady was rather reluctant to obey our captain's command. She did not relish working for a lot of rebels, but seeing that we meant business and intended to have the dinner, she finally got to work and really set up for us a most satisfying repast within a short time.

We saw some very pretty girls in the kitchen, doubtless the daughters of the old lady, squinting at us from time to time, but whenever perceived that we could see them, they "skedaddled" out of sight.

We all sat down to dinner, and expressed ourselves as greatly pleased with the hospitality of the landlady; we told her we should be very glad to see the young ladies, that we were not barbarians, and that they would be surprised to see how nicely we could act towards them, if they would come up and wait on us. The old lady opened the door and cried out, "Come up, girls; these rebel boys are not as bad as you think," and in a few minutes the girls were all up and having a jolly time with us. I think they forgot in a short time that we were enemies of their country and destroyers of their homes. Several flirtations occurred, and all sorts of promises to return after the war were made. These girls were really loath to bid us *adieu*, and waved their handkerchiefs at us as long as we were in sight, and they frequently said, "How could you be so nice and be a rebel?"

Two days later we were drawn up in line of battle in front of Gettysburg. This was the first day's fight. The battle broke over that beautiful valley about three o'clock in the afternoon. Ewell had thrown his men against the Eleventh Army Corps, and by four o'clock the whole Confederate line was driving the enemy before it. General Reynolds was killed in this fight. Captain Bond, leading his company, was among the first to charge into Gettysburg.

General Ewell the next morning appointed Captain Bond provost marshal of the town. We all did active service throughout the entire three days' fight, and on the night of July 4th, the night of the withdrawal of Lee's army from Gettysburg, we were deployed in front of Ewell's line as pickets, to remain in our saddles until relieved. Those of us who were there will never forget that night. The dead had been exposed to the broiling sun for more than twenty-four hours, and had already turned black.

To add to the horror of the scene and the cries and groans of dying men, in the midst of whom we stood, a terrible thunder and lightning storm broke over the battlefield. The rain fell in torrents, and as each of us stood at his post, with pistol in hand, the lightning flashed in our faces casting shadows on the dead strewn around us. Here we remained until day dawned. Who can forget that night! Our sergeant passed down the line, forming us into columns of fours, preparatory to marching off the battlefield.

We continued as General Ewell's bodyguard until we approached Hagerstown, where we rejoined our battalion. In the streets of Hagerstown we encountered a Federal regiment of cavalry, and fought with them in hand-to-hand combat. I shall never forget the magnificent conduct of Sergeant Hammond Dorsey, of our company. With his strong arm he wielded his sabre like Hercules, cutting down many of the enemy from their horses.

We drove them back on the road to Boonesboro', and in another encounter, later in the same evening, our gallant Captain was cut down from his horse with a serious wound in his left leg, compelling his absence from us for several months, while suffering severely from his wound.

We were all "bottled up" with General Lee's army for some days at Williamsport, owing to the high water of the Potomac. General Lee fortified his position, and would have given battle to General Meade if he had attempted to press us beyond this point.

I have a very indistinct recollection of what occurred across the river; in fact, there was no fighting of any consequence. General Lee gradually retired towards Winchester and then to Culpeper, our command extending as far as Fredericksburg on our extreme right.

I was called to Gen. Fitz Lee's headquarters as a courier in the fall of 1863. We were then stationed near Fredericksburg, Colonel Bradley T. Johnson in command of our battalion. I had always wished to serve under Lee, although at that time I knew him only by reputation. The whole cavalry corps looked upon him as an eminently able young officer, and one who would rise rapidly in the estimation of the army.

I felt that I might have a chance here. I certainly did my part, but promotion was slow to Marylanders without friends or influence.

General Lee's headquarters at that time were about three miles distant from Fredericksburg, at Guest's house, on the old plank road.

I suppose I was indebted for this slight elevation to Capt. Henry Lee, brother of Gen. Fitz Lee, a classmate of mine at the University of Virginia prior to the war. From the beginning I formed a most agreeable association with Gen. Lee, his staff, couriers and members of the Signal Corps, which has lasted these many years, and it is a great pleasure to me, whenever the opportunity offers, of coming together with these old comrades. General Lee, recognizing my desire not only to serve my country, but to make for myself a place and position at his headquarters, promoted me, after the Culpeper fight, to the rank of sergeant of the Signal Corps. I participated in all the important engagements which took place during the autumn of 1863, and shortly after the fight at Mine Run, our division went into winter quarters at Charlottesville.

I recall with much pride the magnificent conduct of our cavalry division, under command of Gen. Fitz Lee, in the attack on Kilpatrick's division at Culpeper and Brandy Station; and then again at Buckland, on the Warrenton Road. I could not resist the opportunity of going in with our men in a great charge, which took place in the railroad cut near Brandy Station, where we flanked the enemy. I brought out a Yankee sergeant, who turned over to me a very handsome Colt's revolver, which I presented to General Lee.

Chapter 8

Long Campaigning

Our command, after wintering at Charlottesville, where Gen. Fitz Lee devoted a great deal of time to the reorganization of the cavalry division, to make it more effective in the spring campaign of '64, moved to the vicinity of Fredericksburg.

It was about this time that General Grant, who had assumed command of the Federal forces, and whose intention was to attack General Lee, began his great move to the Wilderness, Chancellorsville and North Anna, culminating in his overwhelming check at Cold Harbor.

The cavalry at this time was most actively engaged guarding both flanks of Lee's army. Our division was thrown in front at Spotsylvania Court House until Longstreet's corps could come up. This was one of the severest fights in which we ever engaged.

We were driven back to the temporary barricade put up by our infantry. It was at this point that Colonel Collins, of the Fifteenth Virginia Cavalry, was killed, and Major Mason and I were ordered by General Lee to bring out his body. There was great confusion at the moment, and we were being pressed to the rear by the advancing line of Federal infantry. I dismounted, and, with the assistance of Mason, tried to lift Collins to my saddle, but failed in doing so, and, under heavy fire, we were compelled to leave him between the battle-lines. After remounting, I had to jump a high barricade, and in the act my horse, a noted piebald stallion, was killed.

General Lee was moving his army by the right flank, chastising Grant severely whenever he attempted to turn it.

We were now constantly engaging the enemy, and were in the saddle day and night. In a little skirmish near Taylorsville, Hanover County, we encountered the Fifth United States Regulars, attacked and routed them. In this fight our handsome young courier, Tom Burke, was shot through the leg, a tender lad of scarcely twenty years, as pretty as a picture, with rosy cheeks. We heard the bullet strike him. It was no joke, but he bore it like a man and behaved like a veteran.

The next day the memorable cavalry fight at Yellow Tavern took place. Sheridan came with overwhelming numbers. We lost the gallant Jeb Stuart, the commander-in-chief of our cavalry, but Sheridan was foiled in his attempt to capture Richmond.

It was a desperate fight along the entire line. General Stuart was wounded and was brought off the field by some of the gallant members of Company K, First Virginia Cavalry. I am proud to say that this company was commanded by Capt. Gus Dorsey, of Howard County, Maryland, and was composed principally of Marylanders.

Major Ferguson, our chief of staff, had his horse shot under him in the fight, and in the confusion the members of our headquarters staff were widely scattered.

I was standing on the Richmond road, our cavalry having just been driven back to the right, when Stuart was wounded. That night I saw him placed in an ambulance. He insisted upon being taken to his wife. I have always felt that Stuart might have lived if he had been kept quiet that night. In a few days the report came of his death. This was a great loss to the country, an irreparable loss to the cavalry. Jackson had died just a year before. Thus two of our greatest commanders had "passed over the river" in so short a time.

On May 23rd we were at Atlee's Station. In the afternoon we moved to Kenyon's farm, on the Lower James, opposite Brandon, for the purpose of breaking up an encampment of negro troops, who had fortified quite extensively at a point known as Harrison's Landing. We reached the place about one o'clock. I had command of headquarter couriers in driving in the pickets and led the charge.

There were about ten of us against a company of negroes on picket. Willie McFarland, of Richmond, Va., a very warm, personal friend of mine, and a member of my signal corps, killed a negro in this charge. The rest surrendered without further resistance.

I carried a message from General Lee, under flag of truce, to the commander of the fort, to surrender. This was refused by Brigadier-General Wild, in command, and I was told to say to General Lee, "Take the fort if you can." This garrison consisted of three regiments of coloured troops, and a number of transports and gunboats were in the river in reserve.

On my return I was asked if the fort could be taken, and I replied that it could not. I had been so close to it, surrounded as it was by a moat, that my mind was quickly made up that any attempt, even to attack, would prove disastrous. However, the order was given to dismount, and two lines formed. As we approached the fort the negroes, with uncovered heads, rose above the intrenchments and levelled their guns upon us. I could see the glint of the sun reflected on their teeth and their polished rifle-barrels. Then came a cloud of smoke, bullets whizzed through our ranks, and the men in our lines tumbled over each other, some forward, some backward. Our fire was ineffective, and they poured volley after volley into our waning ranks. Finally our lines broke and retreated, and we left many dead and wounded on the field. In addition to the effective firing from the fort, several gunboats opened on us, and stampeded our horses. We encamped that night on the Charles City road, near White's Tavern, where we received rations and corn from Richmond.

On May 28th we had a severe fight at Hawes' Shop, where we encountered the enemy in force, and engaged them sharply. We found Yankee cavalry, supported by Yankee infantry, in our front.

The Charleston Dragoons, a splendid body of young men, fresh from their homes, well mounted, became engaged with the enemy. We soon discovered that they were confronted by a line of solid infantry. General Lee sent me to withdraw them. Several of the staff said "Goodbye," as, in obedience to orders, I rode at full speed to the rescue.

Bullets were flying thick and fast, and were thinning out the ranks of this battalion; yet they continued fighting desperately against great odds.

I had not time to address the colonel. I gave the order, as I broke into their ranks, "Right about face, double quick, march," and succeeded in extricating them from a very dangerous position. General Lee complimented me for the prompt manner in which I had acted, and I was also congratulated on all sides on having come out myself unscathed. I think Colonel Rutledge or Colonel Donovan commanded this battalion.

There was no fighting the following day, the division remaining several days in the vicinity of Atlee's Station. During all this time Gen. Robert E. Lee was stubbornly and successfully resisting the efforts of Grant to turn his right flank.

On June first the cavalry moved across the Chickahominy towards

Seven Pines, in the vicinity of Bottom's Bridge. That afternoon both infantry and cavalry became engaged. General Ewell attacking and driving the enemy from his front.

Breckenridge's division came up and we were relieved. On June 3rd there was heavy fighting along the entire line. Grant was handsomely repulsed, and many prisoners were taken. At this time the cavalry had most important service to render, to keep General Lee advised as to whether or not Grant intended crossing the James River, and if so, at what point.

The movement of the cavalry was so rapid in those days that it was a rare thing to find division headquarters wagons up at night. We generally made headquarters at some farmer's house, and these people, although greatly impoverished by the war, always gave us the best they had.

The following day the division was ordered to Ashland, within sixteen miles of Richmond, and here we were joined by Butler's Brigade. We learned that a large force of cavalry, under Sheridan, had encamped the night before at Atlett's, in Caroline County.

The scouts reported that Sheridan's column was marching to join Hunter in the valley. We left Ashland on the afternoon of the 9th, and encamped that night near Trinity Church, made an early start the next morning for Frederickshall, halted there three hours, resumed the march, and encamped at night near Louisa C. H. Sheridan's cavalry encamped within three miles of us.

June 11th we were in the saddle at 3 a. m., encountered the enemy before daylight, and fighting continued throughout the day. I was in the charge that broke Custer's line and captured his headquarters wagons and Colonel Pennington's Horse Artillery.

A few years ago, while visiting Fortress Monroe, I had the pleasure of meeting General Pennington, and of informing him that on that occasion my trophy in the battle was a handsome buffalo robe. I had taken this robe from Pennington's wagon, and I laughingly remarked that, if he still wanted it, there was a lady in Richmond by the name of Miss Mason who would doubtless return it to him.

I also had the pleasure of talking to Captain Green, Custer's adjutant-general, who was captured in this fight, and to whom I extended some slight service on the battlefield.

Some years afterwards I had the pleasure of meeting him in Baltimore. He recalled my kindness to him, remembered my name, and came into my office to meet and thank me again.

Trevilians was a desperate encounter, with varying success to both sides, but finally terminated in Sheridan's retreat.

Hampton followed him in hot pursuit. Our division, however, moved into Trevilians Station the next morning to find a large number of prisoners and wounded men left on the field. Orders were given to establish a hospital and to see that the men received proper attention. Their friends had left them to our care.

That night, after a march of nearly twenty miles, we encamped again in the vicinity of Frederickshall. In speaking of the Battle of Trevilians, I am reminded of many sad memories. Up to this time in almost every engagement in which we fought, we had been successful. We had whipped and routed the enemy upon many a field. Now the tide was turning. No longer had we the men, horses or provender with which to make this branch of the service effective. The history of the cavalry of the Army of Northern Virginia, under Stuart, Hampton and Lee, will, however, stand forever distinguished for its many achievements.

General Sheridan, with inexhaustible resources, was daily adding to his magnificently equipped corps. From this time on we had no means of maintaining our former efficiency. Sheridan was indefatigable, never idle. Within two days we learned he was again on the move. It was almost impossible to keep up with him, and we were on the lookout day and night. The whole line of march was perfumed with dead horses.

It was just at this time that we were experiencing the most trying conditions of the war. On June 23rd we were ordered into saddle at 1 a. m. We moved out across White Oak Swamp, and from thence to Charles City C. H.

A portion of our division that afternoon engaged Gregg's Division. Notwithstanding the excessive fatigue of the men, Gregg was driven back in confusion and pursued for five miles until dark.

Major Breathed, a distinguished Marylander, of whom I shall have more to say later on, killed Colonel Covode, of the Fourth Pennsylvania Cavalry.

In the vicinity of the James River, a malarial country, we suffered from intensely hot weather, and for the want of food and rest, watching Grant's movements, to ascertain at what point he would cross the river or whether he would retreat to Yorktown.

I cannot recall what occurred daily during this hot weather, but we were constantly on the march. About July 1st we crossed the James

River, and marched to Petersburg, and from there to Reams' Station, on the Weldon Railroad.

I now reach a very important cavalry fight. General Wilson, commanding a division of Federal cavalry, was raiding in our rear. We were ordered in pursuit, and were soon in close touch with him. We were brought into action early in the morning, just after Mahone had captured most of his artillery.

We became hotly engaged, forcing the enemy before us, and destroyed most of his wagons, caissons and ammunition. We soon discovered that it was a raid of depredation and cruelty. No respect was paid to private property or to the homes of the defenceless. It developed that more than three thousand negroes were following in the wake of the cavalry and that the majority of the soldiers were loaded with stolen household articles of some kind or other, particularly bed-clothing and wearing apparel. Negro women were seen throwing their little babies ruthlessly aside. Our men became greatly enraged, and it was difficult to restrain them. It was a question of quarter or no quarter, and it was mostly no quarter. I had just returned from the right of our line, where I had witnessed dozens of Yankees shot down in the act of plundering private houses and insulting helpless women, when I hastened to the front with orders from General Lee to keep him advised of what was going on.

I was with Major Breathed at the head of the charging column when he fell wounded. General Lee and Major Ferguson rode up, and everything was done for Breathed that could be done. Fortunately he was not dangerously wounded, although at the time the wound was supposed to be fatal. He rejoined his command within a few weeks. We continued in pursuit of the enemy all day until late at night, camping in the vicinity of Jarratt's Landing. It was a day of horrors. We witnessed the cruelty of warfare in almost every phase. The poor negro women who had left their homes in the hope of obtaining their freedom remained screaming along the roads and in the forests through the night.

As we pressed the enemy, we found the roads strewn with every description of cavalry equipment, wearing apparel, dead men and dead horses, and every variety of stolen property from a negro down to a brooch.

That night, when I was about ready to rest my tired head, Gen. Fitz Lee said: "Gill, I want you to take despatches to Gen. Robert E. Lee, headquarters Appomattox, opposite Petersburg."

I can never forget that night. The stars were shining brightly, but I was in a strange land, and I might say far from home, fully twenty-five to thirty miles from General Lee's headquarters. I told General Lee that it was almost impossible for me to find my way to Petersburg. General Lee said: "You have the best bump of locality of anyone at headquarters. There is the North star; follow it until you reach the Dinwiddie C. H. plank road. Turn sharp to the right, and you will be on the road to Petersburg."

Little did I think what I would have to endure that night. After a ride of a few miles from camp I found the road and the woods resounding with the screams of negro women and the groans of dying men. This made night hideous. I pressed on, however, with my revolver cocked, not knowing at what moment I should be shot down. All kinds of appeals were made to me, but I never stopped. About two o'clock in the morning I crossed the Dinwiddie plank road.

If anything, that night was more trying than the night we stood picket in front of Gettysburg.

I reached General Lee's headquarters about 6:30 in the morning, and delivered my despatches. No one asked me to breakfast. I returned to Reams' Station, about twelve miles away, hungry, tired, and with nothing to eat, reaching camp about noon. Gen. Fitz Lee and his division came up the following day.

A few days later I met Stringfellow, General Lee's popular scout, and in response to an invitation from him, with six or seven other men, I accompanied him on one of his expeditions within the enemy's lines. The first night was spent in the dismal swamp near City Point. We were almost devoured by mosquitoes. Our faces the next morning were badly disfigured. I have always been under the impression that we were lost that night. It was cloudy, and we could not take our bearings, and I think that we sought the swamp for safety. We started early the next morning, and just as we struck the road leading to City Point, we came face to face with a squad of eight or nine Yankee cavalrymen. We charged them at once and routed them, capturing three prisoners. My horse was shot through the neck in the melee but I managed to get back to camp with him. Thus ended this little exploit.

CHAPTER 9

Retreat

On July 29th we broke camp and marched towards Richmond. The next morning we were ordered back, owing doubtless to the explosion of the crater on our lines. We returned to our old encampment near Reams' Station. Here we learned that Hampton was fighting south of us on our right.

Again, on August 5th, we were ordered to Richmond, and continued the march to Ashland. From Ashland we marched across the South Anna River, and encamped late that evening. Here we found recent newspapers from the North, acknowledging the failure of Grant's campaign against Richmond and Petersburg.

The head of our column was turned towards Culpeper; evidently we were again on the march to the Valley. From Culpeper we marched to Flint Hill and across the Blue Ridge at Chester Gap, halting at Front Royal.

Our division met the enemy in the vicinity of Front Royal, but being at headquarters, I did not participate in any fighting.

News came to us on the 20th of August of the death of General Chambliss, who had fallen near Richmond. He was a popular officer, and dearly beloved by everyone.

In the valley General Early was in command of the army, and we remained inactive almost up to the date of the Battle of Winchester. We knew that Sheridan was preparing to move on Winchester. That memorable battle took place on the 19th of September, in which we were badly whipped.

Someone erred in this fight. It seem ridiculous to engage Sheridan with an army of 39,000 opposed to our 12,000 men. Perhaps if Early had kept his three divisions in close touch the result might have been different. I witnessed the entire Confederate line give way. I had been sent to Stevenson's Depot to withdraw Lomax, and we all came back at a gallop with the Yankee cavalry close on our heels.

General Fitz Lee displayed conspicuous gallantry in his efforts to rally the cavalry, and was shot, himself, after having two horses go down under him in quick succession. He was badly wounded. It was almost a miracle that he escaped capture. Had it not been for several members of his staff, who stood by him and got him off the field, he would have been in the hands of the enemy.

Captain Cavendish and I, together with a number of headquarters men, charged at the head of the 6th Virginia Regiment, hoping to check the enemy for the moment to enable the infantry to reform its lines under the gallant Gordon of Georgia.

Sheridan virtually drove us through Winchester, and it would be very difficult for many of us to recall where we slept that night, but we managed to get together the next morning, when, under orders from Major J. D. Ferguson, chief of our staff, we reported to General Wickham, then temporarily assigned to the command of our division.

We never witnessed a worse condition of affairs or worse demoralization among our troops, resulting from the defeat at Winchester, as well as the defeat which followed two days later at Fisher's Hill. Here was a strong position and should have been held, but for some lack of generalship, or for some other reason, Sheridan broke in on our left, precipitating another disastrous rout.

After this experience I always felt like giving a groan when I had to fight under Early. If Gordon had commanded the army, with Fitz Lee commanding the cavalry, the result might have been very different.

The retreat continued up the Valley in the direction of Staunton. We were skirmishing daily. Although only a sergeant in charge of the Signal Corps and our couriers, I managed to make a good impression on General Wickham.

On the morning of the 27th or 28th of September, we were sharply engaged with the enemy near a little town by the name of Vienna, not far from Port Republic. We had just come out of the Luray Valley. The officer commanding the skirmishers was shot down. General Wickham turned quickly to me, and said: "Go, and take command of that line." This was a recognition which I had long sought. In a jiffy I was at my post.

With the exception of myself, the cavalrymen were dismounted. We held the enemy in check, although greatly outnumbered. I had only been there a few minutes when I heard a bullet strike my favourite horse, Red Eye. I scanned his right side, but could not see where the bullet had penetrated. It was all over, however, in a few minutes, when the gallant charger fell to his knees and rolled over on his left side, and I stepped to the ground.

I remained in command until the afternoon. The infantry retired towards Brown's Gap, while the cavalry moved towards Waynesboro ' I was fortunate enough, although under fire, to remove my saddle and bridle and get them to the rear. It was the same old saddle captured in the cavalry charge at Second Bull Run, which I valued very highly.

I got back to headquarters late that night. We encamped near Waynesboro'. Next morning I asked General Wickham for three days' leave of absence to go to Richmond, to get sufficient money to remount myself, which leave was granted.

I arrived in Richmond October 1st, 1864. At that time Confederate money was almost valueless. I succeeded, however, in negotiating a draft for one hundred dollars in greenbacks, payable in Baltimore, for which I received thirty-five hundred dollars in Confederate currency.

I should mention that I had drawn this draft on my mother, who rebuked me in several of her recent "underground" letters for not drawing more frequently. It was my rule, however, never to ask for money from my dear mother unless I was sick, or for some such purpose as just stated.

I had seen the abuse of this privilege early in the war on the part of many gallant Marylanders, who had come South with the best intentions, but who were ruined by dissipation and riotous living at the Confederate capital.

My finances being satisfactorily arranged, I strolled up the main street in Richmond to the Spottswood Hotel. Here I met some old comrades, among whom was George Lemmon. I greeted him most cordially, but was shocked to note the expression of his face. Something surely had happened. Lemmon told me of my brother's death. He had fallen the day before in a desperate encounter with the enemy in front of Reams' Station.

That gallant and heroic band of young Marylanders for the second time, as at Gulp's Hill, had been slaughtered by the enemy. How terrible the blow to me! The dear boy, two years my junior, a lad not yet 20 years of age, the idol of his family, beloved by his comrades and friends, as brave a soldier as ever crossed the Potomac, to die in this way. His body was never recovered. I secured a flag of truce from the

Secretary of War, but like all brave soldiers who die on the ramparts of the enemy's works, he is buried in common with the brave who fell on both sides.

Read what a comrade writes about him:—

One of the gallant dead. Killed in battle by a bullet shot from the hand of the enemy, before Petersburg, Va., September 30th, 1864.

Somerville Pinkney Gill.

He was one of the best soldiers of the Army of Northern Virginia and that ever crossed the Potomac in defence of his oppressed State as well as the noble Confederacy.

He died bravely, he was wounded slightly in the shoulder, and was told by his lieutenant to leave the field. He replied, 'I am only slightly wounded,' and shortly after a bullet pierced his noble forehead and he fell dead.

He would have been taken off by us, but there were so many wounded to look after that we had to leave him in the hands of the enemy. Such is war, and the good and brave boy has gone from us forever.

No name, no record! Ask the world,
The world has read his story.
If all his annals can unfold
A prouder tale of glory.
If ever merely human life
Hath taught diviner moral,
If ever round a worthier brow
Was twined a purer laurel.

Being unsuccessful in my effort to recover my brother's body, I returned to our lines to visit the remaining members of his old company. How few of that gallant band were left! We stood and wept upon each other's shoulders before a word was spoken.

I got back to Richmond the same night. I sought no one. In my room at the Spottswood, buried in inconsolable grief, I sat down to break the news to my dear mother. I struggled for hours over my letter, that I might break the news as gently as possible.

I wished I could say, but I could not say, what some have said:

"*Happily, however, all this is passed, to be seen no more. The fires in that chasm were quenched in Brother's blood.*"

I arrived in Charlottesville on the morning of October 3rd. Here

I secured a remount at the cost of $3,000, but he was not equal to old Red Eye or my piebald stallion, shot under me in the Battle of Spotsylvania.

Leaving Charlottesville immediately, I pressed on to Harrisonburg to rejoin the cavalry. I caught up with them on the 4th, in the neighbourhood of Furrow's Furnace, west of Harrisonburg, and on the road to Warm Springs. Here I found headquarters affairs greatly mixed.

General Wickham had asked for and had been granted a 30 days' leave of absence, and we were ordered to report to General Rosser, now in command of the Division. Rosser learning that the Yankee cavalry was retiring from Harrisonburg, concentrated all his forces and started in pursuit. Rosser made it lively for the cavalry. We had daily encounters with the enemy.

Major Breathed, of the artillery, led in several charges, and returned with his sword red with blood to its hilt. We pressed the enemy down the valley as far as Fisher's Hill, when the Yankees the following day turned tables on us, driving us pell-mell to the rear, flanking us right and left.

Captain Walke, ordinance officer of General Lee's staff, was killed in a gallant attempt to rally the men.

CHAPTER 10

The End is Nigh

It was about this time, during the month of October, 1864, that I was taken sick with my third attack of fever, and ordered to the hospital in Richmond. On the train I met the two Misses Thompson of Staunton, Va., Miss Carter, afterwards Mrs. John Lee Carroll, of Maryland, and her sister, who were exceedingly kind to me, and suggested that instead of going to the hospital, I should try to secure a room at the Arlington Hotel.

This was a valuable suggestion, for here I found my old friend, Mrs. Robert Hough, of Baltimore, Mrs. Gen. Joseph E. Johnston, and several other ladies, who cared for me most tenderly during two weeks of catarrhal fever.

When I got out again I remember a charming visit to Petersburg, visiting Col. George Bolling's family during my convalescence. I felt sufficiently restored in health to rejoin the command, which had gone into winter quarters at Waynesboro'.

In many respects it was an extremely sad and gloomy winter, because the inevitable was upon us. We knew that the spring campaign would end the war with the downfall of the Confederacy.

In the winter of 1864-65 Gen. Fitz Lee intrusted me with the command of a scouting party with orders to reconnoitre the Valley of Virginia, then partly in the hands of the Federal forces under Sheridan.

Sheridan and his army had their winter quarters near Winchester, and it behooved us to exercise the greatest vigilance to escape capture.

I recall spending a night sometime in March at Major Taylor's plantation on the Shenandoah, where we sought refuge owing to a heavy blizzard or snowstorm. During the night the house was surrounded by

Yankees, and if it had not been for a faithful negro man, who assured them that no rebels were there, we should in all probability have been captured.

The old darkey came up into our room, and said the house had been surrounded by Yankees and that we had better get away as soon as we could. One can fancy we were not long in obeying the orders of the old darkey. When we left the house and got into the river road, we heard the clatter of a large cavalry force coming down the road. They evidently knew that we were in the neighbourhood and were not satisfied with their previous investigation. Of course, it was not for us to give them fight but to escape as rapidly as possible, and we dashed off for the nearest ford in the river, to cross over to the mountain side.

We were hotly pursued across the river. Pistol shot after pistol shot was fired at us. Fortunately, however, no one was hurt. It was a bitter cold morning, and the dash through the river wet us to the skin. We galloped a mile or more before reaching a habitation of any kind. Here we stopped to dry our clothes, and to get something to eat and a little apple-jack to drive the frost out of our bones.

An old farmer and his wife were the only occupants of the house, and they did everything for our comfort. We were given a large room with a big hickory fire, and in this way dried our clothes. In a few hours we were in condition to continue the march.

We concluded not to risk another trip into the Valley, which was swarming with patrolling parties of the enemy. There was nothing left for us to do but to go to Upperville, Fauquier County, and to remain there for a few days before deciding on our future course.

I had now only four men with me. Two of the original party had been sent back with despatches to Gen. Fitzhugh Lee. We were most hospitably received at Upperville by the good people of that little village. We made the acquaintance of a charming family by the name of Stephenson. All the old soldiers who had an eye for a pretty girl will doubtless remember Miss Josephine Stephenson. Then the Harrisons and Bollings were nearby, and the Dulanys, on the road to Middleburg, all charming people.

I had the pleasure of being introduced to Captain Glasscock, a captain of Mosby's battalion. I was constantly meeting men of Mosby's command, all splendid fellows, fine horsemen and gallant soldiers. I was very much pleased with the reception I received from everybody. Captain Glasscock invited McFarland and me to his house. The captain had inherited a fine estate from his father a few miles from Upperville, and, to add greatly to the agreeable companionship, we met there the captain who had recently taken to himself a Virginia bride, and we felt that no one could be more fortunate than we were in this opportunity.

Mosby's men were always on the alert, and scarcely a day passed without encountering the enemy at some point. This was only a few weeks before the final surrender at Appomattox.

Glasscock explained to me one morning a little expedition he was getting up to capture a patrol of 22 Yankees, reported as making daily scouts from Georgetown on the road to Vienna in Loudoun County. I gladly availed myself of the opportunity to be with him on this occasion. He took with him about 25 men. Bush Underwood, one of his most trusted lieutenants, was placed in command of the squad which I remained with, while Glasscock, with the rest of the men, took up a position directly on the road about a half-mile beyond where we were hid in the bushes. He would charge them in front, while Underwood would close in rear of the party after they passed the point where we were stationed. It was about midday when the patrol passed up the road. Though they were in full sight of us, we were concealed from them. We waited for the signal from Glasscock to attack, which was one shot from his pistol.

The road was enclosed on both sides by a high fence. The minute the signal was given we dashed into the road, and in a few moments found ourselves face to face with the Yankees in full retreat under fire from Glasscock's pistols. In a moment we were locked together. The entire party was killed or captured with the exception of one officer and two men, who only escaped with fine horses by jumping the fence. In this *mêlée* I unhorsed a Yankee sergeant, and shot him through the right shoulder just as he grappled my horse's reins and levelled his pistol in my face. I had the satisfaction to see him roll in the fence corner, but I held captive his horse, a fine sorrel mare, branded U. S., and it was upon this animal I surrendered a few weeks later.

John Hipkins, of Norfolk, Virginia, rode side by side with me, and when we came back up the road, he claimed that he had shot the man. I put the question to the wounded sergeant, who at once pointed to me as the guilty party.

After this little engagement and my participation in the Harmony fight, which took place a few days later, Captain Glasscock suggested that I be made a lieutenant in Baylor's company, then organizing, if I would remain with Mosby's command. It was quite flattering to me to be offered this position, and I should have been only too well pleased to accept it and serve under so gallant a soldier as Baylor, but I was still under orders from Gen. Fitz Lee, and it was my duty to return to that command at the earliest possible moment. I was particularly desirous to be back with my old cavalry chief, and, if surrender had come, to surrender with those with whom I had been associated for several years.

It was just about this time that my cousin, George M. Gill, who had only a few months before joined Mosby's command, went with Lieut. Wiltshire, and several other young men, to make a scout to Stevenson's Depot.

They were approaching the residence of Col. Daniel Bonham, as a Federal officer, who proved to be Lieutenant Eugene Ferris, of the 30th Mass. Infantry, was seen to pass rapidly from the house to the stable, which was situated in the corner of the yard.

Lieut. Wiltshire and my cousin, who were riding fifty yards in advance of their comrades, passing through the gate which admitted them to the yard, dashed up to the stable door in which Ferris was standing. Without drawing his pistol from the holster, Wiltshire demanded a surrender. "Never with life," replied Ferris, and as Wiltshire was in the act of disengaging his pistol, Ferris inflicted a mortal wound in his neck.

Gill immediately fired, but Ferris standing behind the door post was not struck and at once fired on Gill and inflicted on him a disabling wound. By this time the rest of the party had arrived on the scene of combat.

Ferris received a slight wound and was captured. After the encounter was over, my cousin attempted, notwithstanding his wound, to return to his friends at Upperville, but from the loss of blood was compelled to stop at the house of a citizen in the Blue Ridge. I was informed of his whereabouts and went immediately to him. I found him with a serious wound on the left side of his neck, in close proximity to the jugular vein. Although he was brave and cheerful, I realized the danger at once. I told him that I must be off immediately for a doctor, and bring him some clean clothes. I recall very distinctly that it was a Thursday evening. I promised to be back the following evening.

I rode all night and on my return Friday night I found my dear cousin a corpse. Oh, the horrors of war! Just as I feared, the wound began to slough. The artery gave way and death followed almost immediately. The last word he uttered, as the old mountaineer stood

155

beside him, who had so carefully cared for him was, "I die at least in a good cause."

We buried him Sunday morning in a little graveyard on the mountain side. We dug his grave, and I read a portion of the Episcopal burial service as we put him away. His father came after the war and removed his remains to Baltimore, where they now rest at Greenmount. George Gill was an exceptionally fine character. At college he exhibited unusually fine talent for public speaking, a fine omen of success in the practice of law, which would have been his profession had he lived.

He participated in many of the great battles and was everywhere conspicuous for the highest qualities of a soldier. The day after the second Battle of Manassas he received a severe wound in a skirmish on the Little River turnpike. This compelled him to absent himself from the army until the middle of November.

From that time until after the disaster at Gettysburg he was constantly with Stuart's cavalry, but was taken prisoner at Hagerstown on the retreat of Lee's army. He spent five dreary months in prison, first at Fort Delaware, then at Point Lookout. At the end of this time he was sent to Richmond, and soon after rejoined his regiment, from which he was transferred to Mosby's Partisan Rangers.

The elements in him were finely blended, for manly courage was united with intelligence, a high morality and great gentleness of disposition.

On Fame's eternal camping ground
Their silent tents are spread,
And memory guards with solemn round
The bivouac of the dead.

CHAPTER 11

Surrender!

McFarland and I left Mosby's command sometime about the 8th of April, stopping over a few days at Warrenton. Here we learned for the first time of General Lee's surrender to Grant at Appomattox.

The Richmond papers contained his farewell address to his soldiers of that great Army of Northern Virginia, with whom I had marched and fought for more than four years. I am proud of the privilege of having had my name recorded upon such a muster-roll.

General Lee's last words to his soldiers were to cease fighting, return to their homes and strictly observe their parole until exchanged. Here McFarland and I were at Warrenton greatly perplexed how to decide the next step to be taken. We finally parted at this point. He went to Richmond, where his family resided. I returned to Captain Glasscock's house in Fauquier County. They all welcomed me back, but I brought the sad inevitable news to them, the downfall of the Confederacy.

The next day being Sunday, we all went to church in Upperville, and just as the service was over, someone rode in with a late edition of the Baltimore American, giving full particulars of Lee's surrender and the assassination of President Lincoln.

I think this was about the 16th of April, and the following day copies of General Hancock's proclamation,—who was in command of the Department of the Valley, announcing the surrender of Lee's army and granting to all Confederate soldiers in that locality the same conditions of surrender as had been accorded to Gen. Lee's army, excepting Colonel Mosby, whom they had outlawed, were disseminated through the country.

There was no fighting after this date. Everybody was asking one another what he should do. In discussing the matter with a number of my Maryland comrades I was asked if I intended to accept the terms of surrender and return home. I answered in the affirmative. Everybody was of this opinion, fully realizing that the war was at an end.

It was Sunday, the 23rd of April, just after we had finished dinner at Captain Glasscock's house, where it was our custom to lounge on the grass or sit on the fence smoking our pipes, that our attention was called to several horsemen seen in the distance, crossing the fields in our direction. We soon recognized Col. Mosby and several of his men who were with him.

As Col. Mosby rode up, the conversation turned almost immediately to Gen. Hancock's proclamation. He expressed surprise that anyone should accept such terms. He seemed chagrined that I had already advised some of my friends to do so. I soon found that Capt. Glasscock was thoroughly in accord with the views which I had expressed. Mosby protested against any one leaving his territory at that time. Then it was that I told him I had decided to leave Upperville the following morning and proceed with any of my old comrades who would join me to Gen. Hancock's headquarters, to accept the terms of surrender. I was surprised to find about 20 of Mosby's men in the village, all of whom went with me and were duly paroled. The following day Major Richards, with about 300 of Mosby's men rode into Berryville and accepted the same terms.

Those of us who were Marylanders were permitted by Gen. Hancock to go to Harper's Ferry, and from thence proceed by rail to Baltimore over the Baltimore & Ohio Railroad.

When the train arrived at the Relay House late that evening, within 10 miles of Baltimore, and all were feeling exultant over the prospect of getting home that night, we had our feelings very much disturbed by the entrance into the car of a Federal officer demanding the surrender of our paroles. We declined to give them up. He left the car but soon returned with a squad of soldiers, and ordered us out with fixed bayonets. Of course, we obeyed.

We were imprisoned at the Relay House for more than 10 days. As we had been arrested and held as prisoners without explanation, in violation of the sacred pledge of the government, we felt very much incensed. I finally wrote a letter to General Tyler, then in command at that point, and demanded my release, stating that he had no right to hold me a prisoner, that I had not violated my parole in any way, and that, if I was not to be released, I desired to communicate with my old friend, Mr. Thomas Donaldson, who lived on Lawyer's Hill, and, although a Unionist throughout the war, would see that the wrong was righted and my release secured.

The following morning Gen. Tyler ordered me down under guard to his headquarters. I was told that if I could secure a suit of citizen's clothes from Baltimore, I would be allowed to go into the city.

I asked permission to telegraph to Baltimore, which resulted in getting from Noah Walker & Co., a ready-made suit of clothing, which was sent out to me that afternoon in time for me to return to my family that evening.

Thus ended my four years' experience as a Confederate soldier.

The record of the engagements in which I participated embrace the following historic names: —

First Manassas,	Wilderness,
Front Royal,	Sharpsburg,
Winchester,	Gettysburg,
Bolivar Heights,	Strasburg,
Harrisonburg,	Woodstock
Cross Keys,	Reams's Station,
Seven Days' Battles	Harrison Landing,
Around Richmond,	Hawes Shop,
Cedar Mountain,	Trevilians Station,
Catletts Station,	Yellow Tavern,
Second Manassas,	Brandy Station
Spotsylvania Court House	and Culpeper,

and many other cavalry engagements.

Appendix

Richmond, Va., March 22, 1904.
John Gill, of Baltimore, served at my headquarters and near my side for the greater part of the war from 1861 to 1865. He was one of a number of heroic Marylanders who left their homes to join and do service in behalf of the South.

I had him detailed to report to me because I had been informed that he was a good soldier and performed all the duties confided to him in a satisfactory manner. I first assigned him to duty as a courier, and afterwards promoted him to be sergeant in the Division Signal Corps. I found him active, vigilant, energetic and courageous in the various encounters between my command and the Federal Cavalry. I am correctly quoted as having stated years ago that I would be glad to lead in a fight 5,000 men like John Gill against 10,000 of the enemy.

He should know what he is writing about, because whenever the opportunity occurred his place in the war picture was near the flashing of the guns.

Fitzhugh Lee,
Formerly Major-General Commanding Cavalry Corps of the Army of Northern Virginia.

LEONAUR

ALSO FROM LEONAUR
AVAILABLE IN SOFTCOVER OR HARDCOVER WITH DUST JACKET

AN APACHE CAMPAIGN IN THE SIERRA MADRE *by John G. Bourke*—An Account of the Expedition in Pursuit of the Chiricahua Apaches in Arizona, 1883.

BILLY DIXON & ADOBE WALLS *by Billy Dixon and Edward Campbell Little*—Scout, Plainsman & Buffalo Hunter, *Life and Adventures of "Billy" Dixon* by Billy Dixon and *The Battle of Adobe Walls* by Edward Campbell Little (*Pearson's Magazine*).

WITH THE CALIFORNIA COLUMN *by George H. Petis*—Against Confederates and Hostile Indians During the American Civil War on the South Western Frontier, *The California Column, Frontier Service During the Rebellion* and *Kit Carson's Fight With the Comanche and Kiowa Indians.*

THRILLING DAYS IN ARMY LIFE *by George Alexander Forsyth*—Experiences of the Beecher's Island Battle 1868, the Apache Campaign of 1882, and the American Civil War.

INDIAN FIGHTS AND FIGHTERS *by Cyrus Townsend Brady*—Indian Fights and Fighters of the American Western Frontier of the 19th Century.

THE NEZ PERCÉ CAMPAIGN, 1877 *by G. O. Shields & Edmond Stephen Meany*—Two Accounts of Chief Joseph and the Defeat of the Nez Percé, *The Battle of Big Hole* by G. O. Shields and *Chief Joseph, the Nez Percé* by Edmond Stephen Meany.

CAPTAIN JEFF OF THE TEXAS RANGERS *by W. J. Maltby*—Fighting Comanche & Kiowa Indians on the South Western Frontier 1863-1874.

SHERIDAN'S TROOPERS ON THE BORDERS *by De Benneville Randolph Keim*—The Winter Campaign of the U. S. Army Against the Indian Tribes of the Southern Plains, 1868-9.

WILD LIFE IN THE FAR WEST *by James Hobbs*—The Adventures of a Hunter, Trapper, Guide, Prospector and Soldier.

THE OLD SANTA FE TRAIL *by Henry Inman*—The Story of a Great Highway.

LIFE IN THE FAR WEST *by George F. Ruxton*—The Experiences of a British Officer in America and Mexico During the 1840's.

ADVENTURES IN MEXICO AND THE ROCKY MOUNTAINS *by George F. Ruxton*—Experiences of Mexico and the South West During the 1840's.

LEONAUR

ALSO FROM LEONAUR
AVAILABLE IN SOFTCOVER OR HARDCOVER WITH DUST JACKET

THE LIFE OF THE REAL BRIGADIER GERARD VOLUME 1—THE YOUNG HUSSAR 1782-1807 *by Jean-Baptiste De Marbot*—A French Cavalryman Of the Napoleonic Wars at Marengo, Austerlitz, Jena, Eylau & Friedland.

THE LIFE OF THE REAL BRIGADIER GERARD VOLUME 2—IMPERIAL AIDE-DE-CAMP 1807-1811 *by Jean-Baptiste De Marbot*—A French Cavalryman of the Napoleonic Wars at Saragossa, Landshut, Eckmuhl, Ratisbon, Aspern-Essling, Wagram, Busaco & Torres Vedras.

THE LIFE OF THE REAL BRIGADIER GERARD VOLUME 3—COLONEL OF CHASSEURS 1811-1815 *by Jean-Baptiste De Marbot*—A French Cavalryman in the retreat from Moscow, Lutzen, Bautzen, Katzbach, Leipzig, Hanau & Waterloo.

THE INDIAN WAR OF 1864 *by Eugene Ware*—The Experiences of a Young Officer of the 7th Iowa Cavalry on the Western Frontier During the Civil War.

THE MARCH OF DESTINY *by Charles E. Young & V. Devinny*—Dangers of the Trail in 1865 by Charles E. Young & The Story of a Pioneer by V. Devinny, two Accounts of Early Emigrants to Colorado.

CROSSING THE PLAINS *by William Audley Maxwell*—A First Hand Narrative of the Early Pioneer Trail to California in 1857.

CHIEF OF SCOUTS *by William F. Drannan*—A Pilot to Emigrant and Government Trains, Across the Plains of the Western Frontier.

THIRTY-ONE YEARS ON THE PLAINS AND IN THE MOUNTAINS *by William F. Drannan*—William Drannan was born to be a pioneer, hunter, trapper and wagon train guide during the momentous days of the Great American West.

THE INDIAN WARS VOLUNTEER *by William Thompson*—Recollections of the Conflict Against the Snakes, Shoshone, Bannocks, Modocs and Other Native Tribes of the American North West.

THE 4TH TENNESSEE CAVALRY *by George B. Guild*—The Services of Smith's Regiment of Confederate Cavalry by One of its Officers.

COLONEL WORTHINGTON'S SHILOH *by T. Worthington*—The Tennessee Campaign, 1862, by an Officer of the Ohio Volunteers.

FOUR YEARS IN THE SADDLE *by W. L. Curry*—The History of the First Regiment Ohio Volunteer Cavalry in the American Civil War.